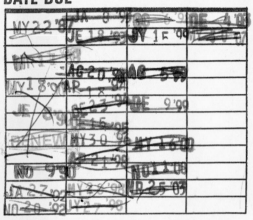

CHELSEA HOUSE PUBLISHERS

Modern Critical Views

Further titles in preparation.

Modern Critical Views

OSCAR WILDE

Modern Critical Views

OSCAR WILDE

Edited with an introduction by

Harold Bloom

Sterling Professor of the Humanities
Yale University

1985
CHELSEA HOUSE PUBLISHERS
New York

THE COVER:

Wilde's self-portrait as the destructive Dorian Gray intimates his sense of both the experiential gain and the spiritual loss brought about by the Aesthetic vision.—H.B.

PROJECT EDITORS: Emily Bestler, James Uebbing
ASSOCIATE EDITOR: Julia Myer
EDITORIAL COORDINATOR: Karyn Gullen Browne
EDITORIAL STAFF: Linda Grossman, Peter Childers
DESIGN: Susan Lusk

Cover illustration by Robin Peterson

Printed and bound in the United States of America

Library of Congress Cataloging in Publication Data

Oscar Wilde.
    (Modern critical views)
    Bibliography: p.
    Includes index.
    1. Wilde, Oscar, 1854–1900—Criticism and interpreta-
tion—Addresses, essays, lectures.   I. Bloom, Harold.
II. Series.
PR5824.08   1985   828'.809   84–28570
ISBN 0–87754–612–6

Chelsea House Publishers
Harold Steinberg, Chairman and Publisher
Susan Lusk, Vice President
A Division of Chelsea House Educational Communications, Inc.
133 Christopher Street, New York, NY 10014

Contents

Editor's Note

This volume gathers, in chronological order of publication, a representative selection of the best criticism devoted to the life and work, the two being inseparable, of Oscar Wilde. It begins with the editor's "Introduction" which emphasizes Wilde's rightness as a critic as being central to his entire achievement. This is followed by an excerpt from the *Autobiographies* of Yeats which gives his personal account of Wilde's catastrophe.

The remaining essays consider the major genres of Wilde's work. Eric Bentley comments upon *The Importance of Being Earnest*, Wilde's acknowledged masterpiece. Edouard Roditi examines Wilde's prose-poems, some of which are almost unique at successfully domesticating into English an altogether French form. G. Wilson Knight, one of the greatest of modern critics, exalts the Wilde of *De Profundis*, audaciously comparing him to Christ. The stage comedies that fall just short of *The Importance of Being Earnest* are analyzed by Epifanio San Juan, Jr.

Two essays by Wilde's most distinguished scholar, the biographer Richard Ellmann, deal with *Salome* and with Wilde's stance as critical theorist, respectively. The volume concludes with a reading of *The Picture of Dorian Gray* by Christopher S. Nassaar.

Introduction

I

Oscar Wilde first published a book in 1881, and after more than a hundred years literary opinion has converged in the judgment that Wilde, as Borges asserts, was almost always right. This rightness, which transcends wit, is now seen as central to the importance of being Oscar. Daily my mail brings me bad poetry, printed and unprinted, and daily I murmur to myself Wilde's apothegm: "All bad poetry springs from genuine feeling." Arthur Symons, like Wilde a disciple of Walter Pater, reviewed the Paterian *Intentions* of Wilde with this exquisite summary: "He is conscious of the charm of graceful echoes, and is always original in his quotations." Symons understood that Wilde, even as playwright and as storyteller, was essentially a critic, just as Pater's fictions were primarily criticism.

Wilde began as a poet, and alas was and always remained quite a bad poet. An admirer of *The Ballad of Reading Gaol* should read the poem side-by-side with *The Ancient Mariner*, in order to see precisely its crippling failure to experience an anxiety of influence. Of course, Ruskin and Pater also began as poets, but then wisely gave it up almost immediately, unlike Matthew Arnold who waited a little too long. It is deeply unfortunate that the young Wilde gave the world this poem about Mazzini:

> He is not dead, the immemorial Fates
> Forbid it, and the closing shears refrain,
> Lift up your heads, ye everlasting gates!
> Ye argent clarions sound a loftier strain!
> For the vile thing he hated lurks within
> Its sombre house, alone with God and memories of sin.

This dreadful travesty and amalgam of Shelley, Swinburne, the Bible, Milton and whatnot, is typical of Wilde's verse, and opened him to many attacks which became particularly nasty in America during his notorious lecture tour of 1882. Thomas Wentworth Higginson, whom we remember as Emily Dickinson's amiable and uncomprehending 'Mentor,' made a public attack upon Wilde's poetic immorality which expanded into an accusation of cowardice for not taking part in the Irish national struggle: "Is it manhood for her gifted sons to stay at home and help work out the problem; or to cross the Atlantic and pose in ladies' boudoirs or write prurient poems which their hostesses must discreetly ignore?" The force of Higginson's rhetoric evaporates for us when we remember that the burly Wilde was no coward, physical or moral, and also when we remember that Higginson, with his customary blindness, linked Wilde to Walt Whitman's work as a wound-dresser in the Washington, D.C. Civil War hospitals: "I am one of many to whom Whitman's 'Drum-Taps' have always sounded as hollow as the instrument they counterfeit." Why, Higginson demanded, had not Whitman's admirable physique gone into battle with the Union armies? A Civil War hero himself, Higginson would have had no scruples about hurling the middle-aged bard and idler into battle. We can credit W. B. Yeats with more insight into Wilde, let alone into Whitman, than Higginson displayed, since Yeats insisted that Wilde was essentially a man of action displaced into a man of letters. In some curious sense, there is a sickness-unto-action in Wilde's life and work, a masked despair that led him to the borders of that realm of fantasy the Victorians called "nonsense" literature, the cosmos of Edward Lear. Lionel Trilling aptly located Wilde's masterpiece, *The Importance of Being Earnest*, in that world, and it seems to me never far from Wilde's work. The metaphysical despair of ever knowing or speaking truth Wilde probably absorbed from his nearest precursor, Walter Pater, whose "Sebastian Van Storck" in *Imaginary Portraits* is a major depiction of intellectual despair. Wilde, deliberately less subtle than his evasive master, Pater, speaks out directly through his mouthpiece, Algernon, in the original, four-act version of *The Importance of Being Earnest*:

> My experience of life is that whenever one tells a lie one is corroborated on every side. When one tells the truth one is left in a very lonely and painful position, and no one believes a word one says.

Wilde's most profound single work is "The Decay of Lying: An Observation," an essay in what now would be called literary theory brilliantly cast in dialogue form. Vivian, speaking for Wilde, rejects what passes for lying in mere politicians:

> They never rise beyond the level of misrepresentation, and actually condescend to prove, to discuss, to argue. How different from the temper of the true liar, with his frank, fearless statements, his superb irresponsibility, his healthy, natural disdain of proof of any kind! After all, what is a fine lie? Simply that which is its own evidence. If a man is sufficiently unimaginative to produce evidence in support of a lie, he might just as well speak the truth at once.

Lying then is opposed to misrepresentation, because aesthetic lying is a kind of supermimesis, and is set, not against truth or reality, but against time, and antithetically against time's slave, nature. As Vivian remarks: "Nothing is more evident than that Nature Hates Mind. Thinking is the most unhealthy thing in the world, and people die of it just as they die of any other disease. Fortunately, in England at any rate, thought is not catching." Nature's redemption can come only through imitating art. We can believe that Wilde's deathbed conversion to the Church was simply a reaffirmation of his lifelong belief that Christ was an artist, not in Wilde a frivolous belief but an heretical one, indeed an aesthetic version of Gnosticism. Hence Wilde's preference for the Fourth Gospel, which he shrewdly regarded as Gnostic:

> While in reading the Gospels—particularly that of St. John himself, or whatever early Gnostic took his name and mantle—I see the continual assertion of the imagination as the basis of all spiritual and material life, I see also that to Christ imagination was simply a form of love, and that to him love was lord in the fullest meaning of the phrase.

This is Wilde speaking out of the depths, in *De Profundis*, the epistle addressed to Lord Alfred Douglas from Reading Gaol. G. Wilson Knight, startlingly linking Wilde and Christ, hints that the ideology of Wilde's homosexuality was its dominant element, involving the raising of love to the high realm of aesthetic contemplation. Without disputing Knight (or Wilde), one can observe that such an elevation is more like Pater than Plato, more like the lying against time that is the privileged moment than the lying against mortality that is the realm of the timeless Ideas. As Pater's most dangerous disciple, Wilde literalizes Pater's valorization of perception over nature, of impression over description.

II

Wilde stands between Pater and Yeats, between a doctrine of momentary aesthetic ecstasies, phantasmagoric hard gemlike flames, and a vision of lyric simplification through aesthetic intensity, what Yeats called the Condition of Fire. Pater, and not Lord Alfred Douglas, was Wilde's disaster, as Yeats knew and intimated. Though his immediate sources were in Ruskin, Swinburne and the Pre-Raphaelites, Pater's sensibility went back to the Keats of the "Ode on Melancholy." Wilde, High Romantic in every way, nevertheless did not have a Romantic sensibility, which is why his verse, derived from all of the Romantics, is so hopelessly inadequate. As a sensibility, Wilde is a fantastic version of Congreve and Sheridan and Goldsmith; an Anglo-Irish wit wandering in the regions of Lewis Carroll, W. S. Gilbert, and Edward Lear, to repeat Trilling's insight again. Nonsense is the truest rejection of mere nature, and the strongest program for compelling nature to cease imitating itself and to imitate art instead. Wilde's theory of criticism achieves magnificence when it extravagantly leaps over sense into the cognitive phantasmagoria of a true theory of the lie, an escape from time into the fantasy of interpretation:

> I know that you are fond of Japanese things. Now, do you really imagine that the Japanese people, as they are presented to us in art, have any existence? If you do, you have never understood Japanese art at all. The Japanese people are the deliberate self-conscious creation of certain individual artists. If you set a picture by Hokusai, or Hokkei, or any of the great native painters, beside a real Japanese gentleman or lady, you will see that there is not the slightest resemblance between them. The actual people who live in Japan are not unlike the general run of English people; that is to say, they are extremely commonplace, and have nothing extraordinary or curious about them. In fact the whole of Japan is a pure invention. There is no such country, there are no such people. One of our most charming painters went recently to the Land of the Chrysanthemum in the foolish hope of seeing the Japanese. All he saw, all he had a chance of painting, were a few lanterns and some fans.

In fact the whole of Japan is a pure invention. There is no such country, there are no such people. That is certainly one of the grand critical epiphanies, one of those privileged moments that alone make criticism memorable. Japan momentarily becomes one with that far and wide land where the Jumblies live, where the Pobble who has no toes and the Dong with a luminous nose dwell together. It is also the land of the Canon Chasuble and Miss Prism and Lady Bracknell, the land of cucumber sandwiches where Wilde deserved and desired to live. Call it, surprisingly enough, what Wilde called it, the land of the highest Criticism:

> . . . I would say that the highest Criticism, being the purest form of personal impression, is in its way more creative than creation, as it has least reference to any standard external to itself, and is, in fact, its own reason for existing, and, as the Greeks would put it, in itself, and to itself, an end. Certainly, it is never trammelled by any shackles of verisimilitude. No ignoble considerations of probability, that cowardly concession to the tedious repetitions of domestic or public life, affect it ever. One may appeal from fiction unto fact. But from the soul there is no appeal.

Call this Wilde's credo, or as Richard Ellmann, his crucial scholar, words it; "The Critic as Artist as Wilde." It leads to an even finer declaration, which catches the whole movement from Ruskin and Pater through Wilde and on to Yeats and Wallace Stevens in their critical essays:

That is what the highest criticism really is, the record of one's own soul. It is more fascinating than history, as it is concerned simply with oneself. It is more delightful than philosophy, as its subject is concrete and not abstract, real and not vague. It is the only civilized form of autobiography, as it deals not with the events, but with the thoughts of one's life; not with life's physical accidents of deed or circumstance, but with the spiritual moods and imaginative passions of the mind.

The only civilized form of autobiography: I know of no better description of authentic criticism. What we want from a critic is not ideology and not method, not philosophy and not history, not theology and not linguistics, not semiotics and not technique, not feminism and not sociology, but precisely the moods and passions of cognition, of imagining, of the life of the spirit. If you want Marx and Hegel, Heidegger and Lacan and their revisionists, then take them, but if you want literary criticism, then turn to Hazlitt and Ruskin, to Pater and Wilde. Wilde's unique gift is the mode of wit by which he warns us against falling into careless habits of accuracy, and by which he instructs us that the primary aim of the critic is to see the object as in itself it really is not.

III

 Why then did Wilde rush to social destruction? On February 14, 1895, *The Importance of Being Earnest* opened in London, only six weeks after the opening of *An Ideal Husband.* Wilde was forty-one, in the full possession of his talents and his health. On February 28, he found the Marquis of Queensberry's card waiting for him at the Albemarle Club, with its illiterate, nasty address "To Oscar Wilde, posing as a somdomite [*sic*]," in which the weird touch of "posing" failed to amuse him. His note of that day to his close friend Robert Ross has an uncharacteristic tone of hysteria:

> Bosie's father has left a card at my club with hideous words on it. I don't see anything now but a criminal prosecution. My whole life seems ruined by this man. The tower of ivory is assailed by the foul thing. On the sand is my life spilt. I don't know what to do.

Had he done nothing he would not have found himself, less than three months later, sentenced to two years' hard labor. Richard Ellmann speaks of Wilde's "usual cycle which ran from scapegrace to scapegoat," and presumably Ellmann's forthcoming biography will explain that compulsion. Whatever its psychopathology, or even its psychopoetics, its most salient quality seems to be a vertigo-inducing speed. Freud presumably would have found in it the economics of moral masochism, the need for punishment. Yeats subtly interpreted it as due to the frustrations of a man who should have spent himself in action, military or political. One remembers Lady Bracknell remarking of Jack's and Algernon's father that, "The General was essentially a man of peace, except in his domestic life," an observation that perhaps precludes any vision of Wilde in battle or in political strife. The economic problem of masochism doubtless had its place within Wilde, but few moralists hated pain more than Wilde, and nothing even in Wilde surpasses the moral beauty of the closing pages of "The Soul of Man under Socialism":

> Pain is not the ultimate mode of perfection. It is merely provisional and a protest. It has reference to wrong, unhealthy, unjust surroundings. When the wrong, and the disease, and the injustice are removed, it will have no further place. It will have done its work. It was a great work, but it is almost over. Its sphere lessens every day.
> *Nor will man miss it. For what man has sought for is, indeed, neither pain nor pleasure, but simply Life.* [Wilde's italics]

We remember, reading this, that Wilde was Ruskin's disciple as well as Pater's. Ruskin's credo, as phrased in *Unto This Last*, is the prophetic basis for Wilde's social vision:

> *There is no wealth but Life*—Life, including all its powers of love, of joy, and of admiration. That country is the richest which nourishes the greatest number of noble and happy human beings.

Why then was the author of "The Soul of Man under Socialism" and of *The Importance of Being Earnest* so doom-eager? His best poem was not in verse, but is the extraordinary prose-poem of 1893, "The Disciple":

> When Narcissus died the pool of his pleasure changed from a cup of sweet waters into a cup of salt tears, and the Oreads came weeping through the woodland that they might sing to the pool and give it comfort.
> And when they saw that the pool had changed from a cup of sweet waters into a cup of salt tears, they loosened the green tresses of their hair and cried to the pool and said, 'We do not wonder that you should mourn in this manner for Narcissus, so beautiful was he.'
> 'But was Narcissus beautiful?' said the pool.
> 'Who should know better than you?' answered the Oreads. 'Us did he ever pass by, but you he sought for, and would lie on your banks and look down at you, and in the mirror of your waters he would mirror his own beauty.'
> And the pool answered, 'But I loved Narcissus because, as he lay on my banks and looked down at me, in the mirror of his eyes I saw ever my own beauty mirrored.'

Kierkegaard might have called this "The Case of the Contemporary Disciple Doubled." Narcissus never saw the pool, nor the pool Narcissus, but at least the pool mourns him. Wilde's despair transcended even his humane wit, and could not be healed by the critical spirit or by the marvelous rightness of his perceptions and sensations.

WILLIAM BUTLER YEATS

The Tragic Generation: Wilde

Shaw and Wilde, had no catastrophe come, would have long divided the stage between them, though they were most unlike—for Wilde believed himself to value nothing but words in their emotional associations, and he had turned his style to a parade as though it were his show, and he Lord Mayor.

I was at Sligo again and I saw the announcement of his action against Lord Queensberry, when starting from my uncle's home to walk to Knocknarea to dine with Cochrane of the Glen, as he was called, to distinguish him from others of that name, an able old man. He had a relation, a poor mad girl, who shared our meals, and at whom I shuddered. She would take a flower from the vase in front of her and push it along the tablecloth towards any male guest who sat near. The old man himself had strange opinions, born not from any mental eccentricity, but from the solitude of his life; and a freedom from all prejudices that were not of his own discovery. "The world is getting more manly," he would say, "it has begun to drink port again," or "Ireland is going to become prosperous. Divorced couples now choose Ireland for a retreat, just as before Scotland became prosperous they began to go there. There are a divorced wife and her lover living at the other side of the mountain." I remember that I spoke that night of Wilde's kindness to myself, said I did not believe him guilty, quoted the psychologist Bain, who has attributed to every sensualist "a voluminous tenderness," and described Wilde's hard brilliance, his dominating self-possession. I considered him essentially a man of action, that he was a writer by perversity and accident, and would have been more important as soldier or politician; and I was certain that, guilty or not guilty, he would prove himself a man. I was probably excited, and did most of the talking, for if Cochrane had talked, I would have remembered an amusing sentence or two; but he was certainly sympathetic. A couple of days later I received a letter from Lionel Johnson, denouncing Wilde with great bitterness. He had "a cold scientific intellect"; he got a "sense of triumph and power, at every dinner-table he dominated, from the knowledge that he was guilty of that sin which, more than any other possible to man, would turn all those people against him if they but knew." He wrote in the mood of his poem, *To the Destroyer of a Soul*, addressed to Wilde, as I have always believed, though I know nothing of the circumstance that made him write it.

I might have known that Wilde's fantasy had taken some tragic turn, and that he was meditating upon possible disaster, but one took all his words for play—had he not called insincerity "a mere multiplication of the personality" or some such words? I had met a man who had found him in a barber's shop in Venice, and heard him explain, "I am having my hair curled that I may resemble Nero"; and when, as editor of an Irish anthology, I had asked leave to quote "Tread gently, she is near under the snow," he had written that I might do so if I pleased, but his most characteristic poem was that sonnet with the lines

Lo! with a little rod
I did but touch the honey of romance—
And must I lose a soul's inheritance?

When in London for my play I had asked news from an actor who had seen him constantly. "He is in deep melancholy," was the answer. "He says that he tries to sleep away as much of life as possible, only leaving his bed at two or three in the afternoon, and spending the rest of the day at the Café Royal. He has written what he calls the best short story in the world, and will have it that he repeats to himself on getting out of bed and before every meal, 'Christ came from a white plain to a purple city, and as he passed through the first street, he heard voices overhead, and saw a young man lying drunk upon a window-sill, "Why do you waste your soul in drunkenness?" He said. "Lord, I was a leper and You healed me, what else can I do?" A little further through the town he saw a young man following a harlot, and said, "Why do you dissolve your soul in debauchery?" and the young man answered, "Lord, I was blind, and You healed me, what else can I do?" At last in the middle of the city He saw an old man crouching, weeping upon the ground, and when He asked why he wept, the old man answered, "Lord, I was dead and You raised me into life, what else can I do but weep?"'"

Wilde published that story a little later, but spoiled it with the verbal decoration of his epoch, and I have to repeat it to myself as I first heard it, before I can see its terrible beauty. I no more doubt its sincerity than I doubt that his parade of gloom, all that late rising, and sleeping away his life, that elaborate playing with tragedy, was an attempt to escape from an emotion by its exaggeration. He had three successful plays running at once; he had been almost poor, and now, his head full of Flaubert, found himself with ten thousand a year:—"Lord, I was dead, and You raised me into life, what else can I do but weep." A comedian, he was in the hands of those dramatists who understand nothing but tragedy.

A few days after the first production of my *Land of Heart's Desire*, I had my last conversation with him. He had come into the theatre as the curtain fell upon my play, and I knew that it was to ask my pardon that he overwhelmed me with compliments; and yet I wonder if he would have chosen those precise compliments, or spoken so extravagantly, but for the turn his thoughts had taken: "Your story in *The National Observer*, 'The Crucifixion of the Outcast,' is sublime, wonderful, wonderful."

Some business or other brought me to London once more and I asked various Irish writers for letters of sympathy, and I was refused by none but Edward Dowden, who gave me what I considered an irrelevant excuse—his dislike for everything that Wilde had written. I heard that Wilde was at his mother's house in Oakley Street, and I called there, but the Irish servant said, her face drawn and tragic as in the presence of death, that he was not there, but that I could see his brother. Willie Wilde received me with, "Who are you; what do you want?" but became all friendship when I told him that I had brought letters of sympathy. He took the bundle of letters in his hand, but said, "Do these letters urge him to run away? Every friend he has is urging him to, but we have made up our minds that he must stay and take his chance." "No," I said, "I certainly do not think that he should run away, nor do those letters advise it." "Letters from Ireland," he said. "Thank you, thank you. He will be glad to get those letters, but I would keep them from him, if they advised him to run away." Then he threw himself back in his chair and began to talk with incoherent emotion, and in phrases that echoed now and again his brother's style at its worst; there were tears in his eyes, and he was, I think, slightly intoxicated. "He could escape, oh, yes, he could escape—there is a yacht in the Thames, and five thousand pounds to pay his bail—well not exactly in the Thames, but there is a yacht—oh, yes, he could escape, even if I had to inflate a balloon in the back-yard with my own hand, but he has resolved to stay, to face it out, to stand the music like Christ. You must have heard—it is not necessary to go into detail—

that he and I have not been friends; but he came to me like a wounded stag, and I took him in." "After his release"—after he had been bailed out I suppose—"Steward Headlam engaged a room at an hotel and brought him there under another name, but the manager came up and said, 'Are you Mr. Wilde?' You know what my brother is, you know how he would answer that. He said, 'Yes, I am Oscar Wilde,' and the manager said he must not stay. The same thing happened in hotel after hotel, and at last he made up his mind to come here. It is his vanity that has brought all this disgrace upon him; they swung incense before him." He dwelt upon the rhythm of the words as his brother would have done—"They swung it before his heart." His first emotion at the thought of the letters over, he became more simple, and explained that his brother considered that his crime was not the vice itself, but that he should have brought such misery upon his wife and children, and that he was bound to accept any chance, however slight, to re-establish his position. "If he is acquitted," he said, "he will stay out of England for a few years, and can then gather his friends about him once more—even if he is condemned he will purge his offence—but if he runs away he will lose every friend that he has." I heard later, from whom I forget now, that Lady Wilde had said, "If you stay, even if you go to prison, you will always be my son, it will make no difference to my affection, but if you go, I will never speak to you again." While I was there, some woman who had just seen him—Willie Wilde's wife, I think—came in, and threw herself in a chair, and said in an exhausted voice, "It is all right now, he has made up his mind to go to prison if necessary." Before his release, two years later, his brother and mother were dead, and a little later his wife, struck by paralysis during his imprisonment; I think, was dead, too; and he himself, his constitution ruined by prison life, followed quickly; but I have never doubted, even for an instant, that he made the right decision, and that he owes to that decision half of his renown.

Cultivated London, that before the action against Lord Queensberry had mocked his pose and his affected style, and refused to acknowledge his wit, was now full of his advocates, though I did not meet a single man who considered him innocent. One old enemy of his overtook me in the street and began to praise his audacity, his self-possession. "He has made," he said, "of infamy a new Thermopylæ." I had written in reply to Lionel Johnson's letter that I regretted Wilde's downfall but not that of his imitators, but Johnson had changed with the rest. "Why do you not regret the fall of Wilde's imitators"—I had but tried to share what I thought his opinion—"They were worthless, but should have been left to criticism." Wilde himself was a martyr in his eyes, and when I said that tragedy might give his art a greater depth, he would not even grant a martyr's enemies that poor merit, and thought Wilde would produce, when it was all over, some comedy exactly like the others, writing from an art where events could leave no trace. Everywhere one met writers and artists who praised his wit and eloquence in the witness-box, or repeated some private saying. Willie Redmond told of finding him, to his astonishment, at the conversazione of some theatrical society, standing amid an infuriated crowd, mocking with more than all his old satirical wit the actors and their country. He had said to a well-known painter during one or other of the trials, "My poor brother writes to me that he is defending me all over London; my poor, dear brother, he could compromise a steam engine." His brother, too, had suffered a change, for, if rumour did not wrong him, "the wounded stag" had not been at all graciously received. "Thank God my vices were decent," had been his comment, and refusing to sit at the same table, he had dined at some neighbouring hotel at his brother's expense. His successful brother who had scorned him for a drunken ne'er-do-well was now at his mercy, and besides, he probably shared, until tragedy awoke another self, the rage and contempt that filled the crowds in the street, and all men and women who had an overabundant normal sexual instinct. "Wilde will never lift his head again," said the art critic, Gleeson White, "for he has against him all men of infamous life." When the verdict was announced the harlots in the street outside danced upon the pavement.

ERIC BENTLEY

"The Importance of Being Earnest"

T he *Importance of Being Earnest* (1895) is a variant, not of domestic drama like *Candida* or of melodrama like *Brassbound*, but of farce, a genre which, being the antithesis of serious, is not easily put to serious uses. In fact nothing is easier than to handle this play without noticing what it contains. It is so consistently farcical in tone, characterization, and plot that very few care to root out any more serious content. The general conclusion has been that Wilde merely decorates a silly play with a flippant wit. Like Shaw he is dismissed as "not really a dramatist at all." Unlike Shaw he does not have any such dramatic structure to offer in refutation of his critics as underlies a *Major Barbara* or a *Candida*. We cannot turn to him for the dialectical steel frame of a Molière or a Shaw. Yet we shall only display our own insensitivity if we dismiss him.

Insensitivity to slight and delicate things is insensitivity *tout court*. That is what Wilde meant when he declared that the man who despises superficiality is himself superficial. His best play is connected with this idea. As its title confesses, it is about *earnestness*, that is, Victorian solemnity, that kind of false seriousness which means priggishness, hypocrisy, and lack of irony. Wilde proclaims that earnestness is less praiseworthy than the ironic attitude to life which is regarded as superficial. His own art, and the comic spirit which Congreve embodied and which Meredith had described, were thereby vindicated. Wilde calls *The Importance of Being Earnest* "a trivial comedy for serious people" meaning, in the first place, a comedy which will be thought negligible by the earnest and, in the second a *comedy of surface* for connoisseurs. The latter will perceive that Wilde is as much of a moralist as Bernard Shaw but that, instead of presenting the problems of modern society directly, he flits around them, teasing them, declining to grapple with them. His wit is no searchlight into the darkness of modern life. It is a flickering, a coruscation, intermittently revealing the upper class of England in a harsh bizarre light. This upper class could feel about Shaw that at least he took them seriously, no one more so. But the outrageous Oscar (whom they took care to get rid of as they had got rid of Byron) refused to see the importance of being earnest.

One does not find Wilde's satire embedded in plot and character as in traditional high comedy. It is a running accompaniment to the play, and this fact, far from indicating immaturity, is the making of a new sort of comedy. The plot is one of those Gilbertian absurdities of lost infants and recovered brothers which can only be thought of to be laughed at. Yet the dialogue which sustains the plot, or is sustained by it, is an unbroken stream of comment on all the themes of life which the plot is so far from broaching. Perhaps *comment* is too flat and downright a conception. Wildean "comment" is a pseudo-irresponsible jabbing at all the great problems, and we would be justified in removing the prefix "pseudo" if the Wildean satire, for all its naughtiness, had not a cumulative effect and a paradoxical one. Flippancies repeated, developed, and, so to say, elaborated almost into a system amount to something in the end—and thereby cease to be flippant. What begins as a prank ends as a criticism of life. What begins as intellectual high-kicking ends as intellectual sharp-shooting.

The margins of an annotated copy of *The Importance* would show such headings as: death; money and marriage; the nature of style; ideology and economics; beauty and truth; the psychology of philanthropy; the decline of aristocracy; nineteenth-century morals; the class system. The possibility of such notations in itself means little. But if we bear in mind that Wilde is skimming steadily over mere topics all through *The Importance*, we can usefully turn to a particular page to see precisely how this works. To choose the opening page is not to load the dice in a dramatist's favor, since that page is usually either heavy-going exposition or mere patter which allows the audience to get seated. Here is Wilde's first page:

ALGERNON: Did you hear what I was playing, Lane?

LANE: I didn't think it polite to listen, sir.

ALGERNON: I'm sorry for that, for your sake. I don't play accurately— anyone can play accurately—but I play with wonderful expression. As far as the piano is concerned sentiment is my forte. I keep science for life.

LANE: Yes, sir.

ALGERNON: And, speaking of the science of Life, have you got the cucumber sandwiches cut for Lady Bracknell?

LANE: Yes, sir.

ALGERNON: Oh! . . . by the way, Lane, I see from your book that on Thursday night, when Lord Sherman and Mr. Worthing were dining with me, eight bottles of champagne are entered as having been consumed.

LANE: Yes, sir; eight bottles and a pint.

ALGERNON: Why is it that at a bachelor's establishment the servants invariably drink the champagne? I ask merely for information.

LANE: I attribute it to the superior quality of the wine, sir. I have often observed that in married households the champagne is rarely of a first-rate brand.

ALGERNON: Good heavens! Is marriage so demoralizing as that?

LANE: I believe it *is* a very pleasant state, sir. I have had very little experience of it myself up to the present. I have only been married once. That was in consequence of a misunderstanding between myself and a young person.

ALGERNON: I don't know that I am much interested in your family life, Lane.

LANE: No, sir. It is not a very interesting subject. I never think of it myself.

ALGERNON: Very natural, I am sure. That will do, Lane, thank you,

LANE: Thank you, sir. (*He goes out*)

ALGERNON: Lane's views on marriage seem somewhat lax. Really, if the lower orders don't set us a good example, what on earth is the use of them? They seem, as a class, to have absolutely no sense of moral responsibility.

This passage is enough to show the way in which Wilde attaches a serious and satirical allusion to every remark. The butler's "I didn't think it polite to listen, sir" is a prelude to the jokes against class society which run through the play. Algernon's first little speech touches on the foolish opposition of life and sentiment, science and art. Talk of science and life leads by Wildean transition back to the action and the cucumber sandwiches. Champagne takes the action to speculation on servants and masters, and thence to marriage and morals. A little dialectical climax is reached with the answer to the question: "Is marriage so demoralizing as that?" when Lane coolly replies: "I believe it *is* a very pleasant state, sir," and adds, by way of an explanation no less disconcerting by Victorian standards, "I have had very little experience of it myself up to the present. I have only been married once." Which is followed by the explanation of the explanation: "That was in consequence of a misunderstanding. . . ." It cannot be said that marriage in this passage receives the "staggering blows" which the ardent reformer is wont to administer. But does it not receive poisoned pin pricks that are just as effective? Are not the inversions and double inversions of standards managed with dexterous delicacy? "No, sir. It is not a very interesting subject." A delicious turn in the argument! And then the little moralistic summing-up of Algernon's: "Lane's views on marriage seem somewhat lax. Really, if the lower orders don't set us a good example . . ." And so it ripples on.

We are accustomed to plays in which a serious plot and theme are enlivened—"dramatized," as we say—by comic incident and witticism. Such plays are at best sweetened pills. "Entertainment value" is added as an afterthought, reminding one of the man who, having watched for weeks the construction of a modern Gothic building, cried one day: "Oh, look, they're putting the architecture on now!" Oscar Wilde's procedure is the opposite of all this. He has no serious plot, no credible characters. His witticisms are, not comic, but serious relief. They are in ironic counterpoint with the absurdities of the action. This counterpoint is Wilde's method. It is what gives him his peculiar voice and his peculiar triumph. It is what makes him hard to catch: the fish's tail flicks, flashes, and disappears. Perhaps *The Importance* should be defined as "almost a satire." As the conversations in *Alice in Wonderland* hover on the frontier of sense without ever quite crossing it, so the dialogue in *The Importance* is forever on the frontier of satire, forever on the point of breaking into bitter criticism. It never breaks. The ridiculous action constantly steps in to prevent the break. That is its function. Before the enemy can denounce Wilde the agile outburst is over and we are back among the cucumber sandwiches.

The counterpoint or irony of Wilde's play expresses itself theatrically in the contrast between the elegance and *savoir-faire* of the actors and the absurdity of what they actually do. This contrast too can be dismissed as mere Oscarism and frivolity. Actually it is integral to an uncommonly rich play. The contrast between smooth, assured appearances and inner emptiness is, moreover, nothing more nor less than a fact of sociology and history. Wilde knew his England. He knew her so well that he could scarcely be surprised when she laughed off his truisms as paradoxes and fastened a humorless and baleful eye on all his flights of fancy. Wilde had his own solution to the problem stated by Meredith, the problem of finding a vantage point for satire in an unaristocratic age. It was the solution of Bohemianism. For Wilde the Bohemian attitude was far from being a philosophy in itself—a point which most of his friends and enemies, beginning at the Wilde trial, seem to have missed. Bohemianism was for Wilde a mask. To wear masks was Wilde's personal adjustment to modern life, as it was Nietzsche's. Hence we are right in talking of his pose as we are right in talking of Nietzsche's vanity. The mistake is in believing that these men deceived themselves. If we patronize them the joke is on us. If Wilde seems shallow when we want depth, if he seems a liar when we want truth, we should recall his words: "A Truth in Art is that whose contradictory is also true. The Truths of metaphysics are the Truths of masks."

EDOUARD RODITI

The Poems in Prose

For their form and type of content, Wilde's prose poems are much indebted to Baudelaire and to Pierre Louÿs, one of Wilde's Paris friends who probably helped him write the original French text of *Salome* and to whom the play was dedicated. Other French influences that determined the nature of Wilde's prose poetry were those of Flaubert, Théophile Gautier, Marcel Schwob and Rémy de Gourmont. From Flaubert was derived the plot of *Salome*, which is based on his *Hérodias*; and his descriptive style, in this work as well as in *Salammbo* or *La Tentation de Saint Antoine*, was a valuable element in Wilde's elaboration of a mythopoeia or "art of lying." To Gautier, Wilde owed other aspects of his art of describing the imagined or the unreal in concrete terms that appeal to the senses of perception; and to Marcel Schwob and Gourmont, theorists and masters of the more learned circles among the French decadents, he owed much of his interest, as to Flaubert too, in all the Asiatic or Alexandrine elements of antiquity to which he had not been initiated by Walter Pater. Of this manner, *La Sainte Courtisane*, on a theme which Anatole France, another friend of Louÿs, developed more fully in *Thaïs*, is a typical example. The transition from *Charmides* to this antiquity of which *The Sphinx* is also part, is as striking, in Wilde's work, as it is, in the history of taste, from the neo-classical antiquity of Addison's *Cato* to that of *Marius the Epicurean*, of *Quo Vadis* or of *The Last Days of Pompeii*; in painting, a similar transition illustrated in the shift from the antiquity of Lord Leighton to that of Gustave Moreau.

An interest in magic, in religious mysteries and in Gnostic or Early Christian beliefs was prominent in the antiquarian scholarship of Oscar

Wilde and the French decadents. It was primarily an interest in aspects of antiquity that Renaissance Humanism had neglected, in all that was obscurely irrational or barbaric or Christian, popularly superstitious or Asiatic rather than luminously classical and rational, in all that was Carthaginian, Persian, Egyptian or Etruscan and that official Athenian or Roman culture had submerged, in the archaic elements that classical culture had concealed. In discovering the beauty of such poetry as the early Latin chorus of the Arval Brotherhood or the popular songs of the ancient world and its magical formulae and incantations, the scholars and esthetes of the last decades of the Nineteenth Century had to reject many of the critical principles of Classicism. In their stead, they relied on the sublime and concluded that it resided to a great extent, in such poetry, in the hallucinatory power of vivid description of objective detail or in the obsessive intensity of repetition and of strict patterns of syntax. It is significant, in this respect, that the earliest known discussion of the sublime should be that of Longinus, an Asiatic Greek of the post-classical era when cultured Greeks had begun to understand and appreciate the thought and art of such "barbarians" as the Egyptians and the Hebrews; and that Longinus should even quote the *Book of Genesis* as an example of the sublime, which no critic in Periclean Athens would have deigned to do.

Baudelaire had similarly stressed the mysterious beauty of medieval Latin poetry, and even imitated, in *Franciscae meae Laudes* and elsewhere, its puns and verbal patterns; and Rimbaud, in *A Season in Hell*, confessed his love for Church Latin. All these tastes of the later Romantics, Decadents and Symbolists, for post-classical Greek and Latin poetry, had finally been fused, together with other beliefs, in a new poetics whose aims partook both of thaumaturgy and of psychopathology. On the one hand, those who tended toward Rimbaud's verbal alchemy sought, by vividly descriptive writing, to create the illusion of the thing that the word symbolizes; the poet thus became a magician, emulating God, as some poets and estheticians had suggested from Tasso to Novalis, in his creation of a world that was born of his poem. On the other hand, by obsessive rhythms and alliterations or imagery, the poet sought to hypnotize his reader, to project upon him, as Poe intended, specific moods or emotions; and he thus became, in a way, a psychopathologist or at least a dabbler in theories of madness and of suggestion. The communion of poet and reader, in magic or madness, was achieved through some element that transcends reason, through the sublime; and the chief devices of the sublime, it seems, were vividly descriptive and hallucinatory or obsessively repetitive and rhythmical, the *diatyposis* and the *anaphora* of Longinus.

The declamatory prose-poetry of *Salome* illustrates Oscar Wilde's contribution to this new art of poetry. Even in the English translation, which no longer communicates the carefully chosen rhythm and imagery of the original French, the obsessive pattern of the repetitions and the hallucinatory quality of the descriptions are clearly apparent: "The moon has a strange look tonight. Has she not a strange look? She is like a mad woman, a mad woman who is seeking everywhere for lovers. She is naked too. She is quite naked. The clouds are seeking to clothe her nakedness, but she will not let them. She shows herself naked in the sky. She reels through the clouds like a drunken woman. . . . I am sure she is looking for lovers. Does she not reel like a drunken woman? She is like a mad woman, is she not?" Here, the repetitions communicate Herod's own obsessive melancholia, whose nature is strikingly symbolized in the imagery: and when Salome later dances before him, she embodies his obsession even more vividly than the moon.

The forms of such prose poetry illustrate clearly how Neo-Platonist and Romantic esthetics; by stressing the quality of the sublime in poetry and by neglecting all the more formal principles and elements of Aristotelian and Horatian criticism, had inevitably reached the conclusion that the sublime could exist in prose as well as in poetry. Longinus had already discussed the orator's sublime in the same arguments as the poet's sublime, never clearly distinguishing the one from the other. Prose was thus as legitimate a form of poetry as any verse-form; and the more formal artists of the second generation of French Romantics therefore began to experiment consciously with prose poetry and to develop, for the prose poem, forms that were more strict than the rhapsodic prose of Chateaubriand or Volnay, and more closely allied, by curious analogies, to the verse-forms with which these poets were most familiar. By stripping poetry of its structure of rhythm and rhyme, Baudelaire soon reduced it, in his prose poems, to its elements of factual content, plot and atmosphere; and his poetics of the prose poem have much in common with those of the fantastic tales of Poe, or of the prose translation of a poem. Rimbaud, a few decades later, neglected the element of fact or of plot which had sometimes made Baudelaire's prose poems almost journalistic, too much like sketches or short stories; instead, Rimbaud developed the lyrical element of atmosphere, till his prose *Illuminations*, by using all the same devices of diction, syntax and imagery as the verse *Illuminations*, achieved the same elliptical and mysterious perfection.

Oscar Wilde does not seem to have known Arthur Rimbaud's prose poetry, but to have borrowed the esthetics of prose poetry from Baudelaire and a few of his less experimental followers, especially from Pierre Louÿs, whose *Chansons de Bilitis* imitate the manner and forms of translations of late Greek lyrical poems. Before Baudelaire, Aloysius Bertrand, the earliest master of the French prose poem, seems likewise to have imitated, in *Gaspard de la Nuit*, the forms of prose translations of German ballads or of medieval lyrics. In a curious fragment generally printed erroneously as a preface to *A Season in Hell*, Rimbaud had indeed parodied the *New Testament*, much as Wilde did in some of his *Poems in Prose*; and traces of imitation of Biblical style can be found elsewhere in Rimbaud's work. But Rimbaud and Wilde had a common source, in Baudelaire and in the vast Biblical and Satanic literature of Romanticism; both the style and the irony were thus common property, no valid proof that Wilde knew Rimbaud's work.

In English literature, the prose poem has never obtained the same recognition, as a legitimate form of poetry, as in France. No English or American poets of the importance of Baudelaire or Rimbaud have sponsored it in the past, and no school as fruitful as that of Apollinaire or of the Surrealists has made an issue of it in our age. Wilde's *Poems in Prose* thus have something freakish or awkward about them; they follow no known English patterns and must create, as they go, a form that has not been generally imitated, except by such crude or popular writers as Kahlil Gibran, much as Poe's poetic and narrative forms were imitated by jingle-bell rhymesters and pulp-magazine hacks. The *Poems in Prose* now suggest too clearly the forms of non-poetic or pseudo-poetic prose. The more Biblical ones, with their studied archaisms, sound like translations; and *The Artist* or *The Disciple* are like expanded epigrams. Finding no other bronze available, the artist fashions his new image, "The Pleasure that abideth for a moment," out of his earlier image, "The Sorrow that endureth for ever"; and the pool mourns Narcissus, not because he gazed so faithfully into its depths, but because it had always contemplated its own beauty reflected in the youth's eyes. In all this, there seems to be too much wit; the devices of diction and of plot or structure are too apparent, and there is not enough of the lyrical atmosphere of true poetry.

But the very nature of the wit in the Biblical *Prose Poems* illustrates Wilde's constant preoccupation with themes of guilt and sin. In the artist's development, this preoccupation reveals itself esthetically as a haunting sense of inadequacy, a striving toward an even greater purity of form or content. Wilde was never, as some artists seem to be, satisfied with any of his art. His refusal to rewrite *Vera*, for instance, because it was "a work of genius," in fact all his boasting and exhibitionism can thus be interpreted as manifestations of an ambivalent defense-mechanism, the purpose of which was to silence any critics who might be tempted to affirm what his own artistic conscience never ceased suggesting; or else, to force them to state it openly and thus free him from the anguish of doubt. And Wilde constantly refined his art by banishing, from each genre that he attempted, all elements that proved to be better suited to other genres. From his poetry, he banished all the essayistic thought, the politics, the ethics and the esthetics of such earlier works as *Eleutheria, Humanitad* or *The Garden of Eros*, and most of the decorative and descriptive art of his Pre-Raphaelitic manner, its archaeological or historical reconstruction, till he achieved the almost pure poetry of *The Harlot's House*. He likewise stripped his lyrical drama of much that had marred *Vera*, the unnecessary devices and incidents of plot and the pseudo-realistic detail, for instance, till the genre was reduced to its basic elements in *Salome*. As Wilde sorted his varied gifts, he was able to discover, in his study of each genre, the aspects of his personality which could be cultivated there most fruitfully and which, by their very number and conflicting natures, destroyed the unity of his less experienced work. The element of wit and paradox which still rings so false in some of the *Poems in Prose* was thus something that Wilde later rejected, when he refined his prose poetry enough to permit the writing of *Salome*.

In his earlier poems, Wilde had already expressed his sense of guilt in ethical terms and with less self-knowledge, as in *Humanitad*:

> By our own hands our heads are desecrate . . .
> And we were vain and ignorant nor knew
> That when we stabbed this heart it was our own
> real hearts we slew.

Elsewhere, in the early poems, Wilde had proclaimed, as in *Ravenna*, that "The woods are filled with gods we fancied slain," or that "all thoughts of black Gethsemane" were drowned; and he had even spoken contemptuously, in *The Burden of Itys*, of "One I some time worshiped." But the "fond Hellenic dream" of his youthful paganism had apparently proved false; and Wilde slowly returned to Christianity, though to a curiously Alexandrine or Hellenistic heterodoxy which, in *Salome*, the *Poems in Prose* or the fairy-tales, adopted Biblical diction and forms, such as the parable, to illustrate a paradoxical ethics of good and evil whose Manichaean identity of contraries is typical of many heresies that once flourished among the more Oriental sects of Gnosticism and Early Christianity.

Nor is this development, from decadent paganism and hedonism to mystical Christianity, at all unusual. It is illustrated in the very history of the ancient world's decline and fall, and in the many legends of pagan sinners who converted and became saints; and several other nineteenth-century decadents who had tried to revive the hedonism and paganism of late antiquity found that these led them almost inevitably back to the Christianity which they had first rejected, though to a more mystical form of it. The most outstanding disciple of the neo-pagan painter Gustave Moreau has thus been the Catholic mystic Georges Rouault; and Wilde's own art, which borrowed so many pagan elements, in *The Sphinx* or *Salome*, from the paintings of Gustave Moreau, also rejected these symbols guiltily, in the last lines of *The Sphinx* and especially in the paradoxical cult of sin which distinguishes much of his later work, from the *Poems in Prose* and *The Harlot's House* to *The Ballad of Reading Gaol* and *De Profundis*. In Baudelaire, in Wilde and in Rouault, the same Manichaean Christianity leads indeed to the same apotheosis, through sins redeemed, of the prostitute, the spiritual counterpart, in knowledge and rejections of evil, of the saint whom evil has never touched. And the paradox thus becomes an illustration of the Crucifix, its cross-purposes torturing the artist or the mystic with both doubt and certitude.

Paradox and antithesis can suggest, in an *a priori* synthesis analogous to much dialectical reasoning, what cannot be stated logically; and this ineffable of the mystic's intuition of the identity of contraries is analogous, in a different area of experience, to the mathematician's intuition of the infinite or the esthetician's of the sublime. The weakness of Wilde's *Poems in Prose*, as poetry, thus lies in their paradoxical content, which is of an ethical or theological nature rather than of an esthetic nature, so that they express an ineffable rather than a sublime. And a painter such as Rouault has thus solved the esthetic problem of Manichaeanism, with its dualism of good and evil, far more adequately than Wilde: he achieves the sublime in ugliness, beauty in the grotesque, art's equivalent of the body's experiencing the Heraclitean or Taoist identity of contraries in the pleasure of pain.

In *The Master*, among the Biblical *Poems in Prose*, Joseph of Arimathea meets, on the day of the Crucifixion, a young man who is weeping, his body wounded with thorns and his head strewn with ashes. The young man declares: "It is not for him that I am weeping, but for myself"; he has performed the same miracles as Christ and bitterly resents not having been similarly crucified. His plight is indeed that of the many other Messiahs of the age of the Gospels, when some heretical or Essenian sects even believed that Christ was but the supreme Messiah amongst many, and that one of these other Messiahs was to be found living in each age; and Cabbalist Jewish doctrine still distinguishes an ever-present Messiah, Son of Joseph, whose avatars are continuous as those of the Dalai Lama, from the Messiah, Son of David, who is to be the real and last Messiah. In another prose poem *The Doer of Good*, Wilde portrays a

Messiah who discovers that all those whom he has miraculously healed have not morally benefited thereby: the former leper has become a voluptuary, the blind man a lecher, the woman whose sins had been forgiven has started a new life of sin, and the man raised from the dead now spends his days mourning. In a world of the flesh, there is no escape from the sin and sorrow of the flesh.

These *Poems in Prose* expound indeed too much doctrine; they almost fall into what Wilde, in his review of the English translation of Chuang Tzu's Taoist classic, calls "the vulgar habit of arguing." It is elsewhere that Wilde's real prose poetry is to be found, in some of his fairy-tales, in *Salome* and in the myths that glitter like jewels in the dialectical setting of his dialogues. The dialogue on *The Decay of Lying* thus contains a brilliant illustration of the use and purpose of the myth and, at the same time, of the sort of unconditional surrender that Wilde's *Magister* expects, in the dialogues, of his *Discipulus* and of the reader, or that one character, in his lyrical dramas, expects of the other characters and of the audience. When tragedy or dialogue no longer distinguish structurally, in their rhetorical devices, the participants from the public, they can no longer purge the passions of the heart or the errors of the intellect; and they must then depend on the magic spell and total acquiescence which the sublime engenders rather than on the *catharsis* which the more persuasive or argumentative arts of *dianoia* and dialectical elucidation facilitate by moving the passions or exercising the understanding.

In *The Decay of Lying*, Vivian is arguing that the aim of art and of lying is to charm, and that the Truth in art is a matter of style, not of mere fact. But Cyril, the *Discipulus*, is not prepared to believe his *Magister*. Vivian then abandons all argument and illustrates his theory in a vividly descriptive allegory; "Art finds her own perfection within, and not outside of, herself. She is not to be judged by any external standards of resemblance. . . . She has flowers that no forests know of. . . . The dryads peer through the thicket as she passes by. . . . She has hawk-faced gods that worship her, and the centaurs gallop at her side." At this point, Cyril interrupts Vivian, more charmed than persuaded by the descriptive imagery: "I like that. I can see it. . . ."

In the same manner, Wilde convinces his readers more completely, as a poet in prose, only when his imagery and his descriptions of the unreal are most objectively vivid, in some passages of *Salome*, for instance, in the best of his fairy-tales and in the myths of his dialogues. Here Wilde's prose poetry follows esthetic principles that are better suited to his temperament than those of Baudelaire's prose poetry, which Wilde imitated almost too schematically, making it seem bare and impoverished rather than adorned and enriched as Rimbaud did. But these new principles established no forms for the prose poem; instead, they developed a poetical manner, an aura of the sublime which was intended to emanate from the whole poem, whatever its form. Of the prose sublime, Wilde already knew magnificent examples in English, in the prose of Ruskin, "whose rhythm and color and fine rhetoric and marvellous music of words are entirely unattainable," and of Walter Pater, "who through the subtle perfection of his form, is inimitable absolutely," or in the prose of Landor and De Quincey and in the Oriental fantasies of Beckford's *Vathek*; and declamatory invocations or descriptions, such as that of Chateau Désir in *Vivian Grey* or those that embellish *Melmoth*, had been, ever since *The Castle of Otranto*, one of the main features of the gothic novel. In French too, there was an older tradition of such rhapsodic prose, in the works of Volnay or Chateaubriand, and especially in Maurice de Guérin's evocation of mythical antiquity, *Le Centaure*, to which Wilde's own visions of Arcady were so closely allied. In one of his book-reviews, Wilde had even written: "It is not that I like poetical prose, but I love the prose of poets."

In his fairy-tales, Wilde perfected, to a great extent, his poet's prose, and in much the same manner as he perfected his art in other genres too. The earlier tales, those of the volume that contains *The Happy Prince*, still aim at too many artistic objectives; their pathos is of a more conventional sort than their descriptive art, and their humor too self-conscious for their fantasy. Animals, plants and inanimate objects here reason and talk and behave like human beings; and human beings, such as the student in *The Nightingale and the Rose*, are oddly obtuse and insensitive, no more human than the water-rat of *The Devoted Friend* or the inanimate hero of *The Remarkable Rocket*. In all this satire, human beings, animals and inanimate objects think and talk the same selfish language, except the swallow and the statue in *The Happy Prince* or the nightingale in *The Nightingale and the Rose*; but there is something arbitrary and strained in the almost foolish virtue of the few hero-victims, something too contrived in the pathos and the moral of each tale, too much of the schematic in the many shifts from one level of art to another, from the simplicity of tales written for children to the witty artifices of adult irony and satire, and in the shifts from one artistic objective or special audience to another.

In an introduction to Wilde's collected fairy-tales, W. B. Yeats once wrote: "The further Wilde goes in his writings from the method of speech, from improvisation, from sympathy with some especial audience, the less original he is, the less accomplished. . . . *The Happy Prince and Other Tales* is charming and amusing because he told its stories. . . . A

House of Pomegranates is overdecorated and seldom amusing because he wrote its stories." To the Papas and Mamas of the upper-class nurseries of the late Victorian era, such moral tales as *The Happy Prince, The Selfish Giant, The Devoted Friend, The Nightingale and the Rose* or *The Remarkable Rocket,* with their elaborate pathos, sly satire and coy humor, were charming and amusing; and Yeats, who shared some of their rather patronising views concerning the tastes and reasoning of children as mere miniature adults, assumed that Wilde's earlier fairy-tales were perfectly adapted to a childish audience, though they have always been more popular with adult readers than with children. But children are lovers of straight narrative, and generally resent the suspense and delays of a more sophisticated arabesque of ironies; and it is a symptom of a peculiar perversion of taste, in our age that feels such a great nostalgia for the irresponsibilities of childhood, that so many adults should delight in a literature which only pretends to be written for children and still uses many of the devices of adult thinking.

In Wilde's writings, this adult imitation of childish thinking illustrates an attempt to overcome, by making a virtue of it, some deeply-rooted awkwardness or sense of guilt as an artist; and Wilde tried to overcome the same inhibitions, in other works, by imitating the styles of translation or the Biblical manner. What Yeats admired, in the earlier fairy-tales, was thus no genuine simplicity, no close rendering of the patterns of Wilde's conversational style, which was always elaborately paradoxical and richly descriptive, but an affectation of simplicity; Yeats quite properly resented, however, some of the descriptive imagery, the "fair pillars of marble," the "loud music of many lutes," the "hall of chalcedony and the hall of jasper" and all the other decorative props which recur so frequently when, in his attempt to emulate the painter's art and thus stimulate the reader's visual imagination, Wilde lapses into careless repetition or hasty description of the same floral pieces, the same imitation antique or semi-precious stones. The fabulous conversations of animals and flowers, in the garden of *The Nightingale and the Rose*, are thus repeated, in a way, in *The Birthday of the Infanta*, when the dwarf wanders into the garden; and *Salome* repeats much of the description of the Biblical *Poems in Prose.*

At his best, in the later tales of *A House of Pomegranates,* Wilde really achieved, in some descriptions, the magic effects which were his real objective; there, his art of lying creates and describes mythically what does not exist, and charms and convinces as utterly as if it did exist. In the Oriental scenes of *The Fisherman and his Soul,* some details of description are perhaps unnecessary to the story. But these arbitrarily introduced details, the woman "who wore a mask of gilded leather," the mountains where "we held our breath lest the snow might fall on us, and each man tied a veil of gauze before his eyes," the strange places and things and people, "the Aurantes who bury their dead on the tops of trees," all these, because each in turn is so exotic and new and surprising, introduce into the story an element of the fantastic or the sublime which Wilde had found in Herodotus, in Mandeville or in Marco Polo and which, while we now read him, we can still see much as Cyril, in *The Decay of Lying*, saw the "hawk-faced gods" of Vivian's allegory.

This is the great art of Wilde's poetic prose, achieved only, among the fairy-tales, in the best of *The House of Pomegranates*, in parts of *The Birthday of the Infanta*, *The Young King* or *The Star Child*, and in the whole of *The Fisherman and his Soul*; here, the richness of style and description is not affected, as was the Elizabethan pastiche of *Vera*, nor wearisome, as are some of the floral descriptions in Wilde's earlier poems or the catalogues of rare objects in *The Picture of Dorian Gray*. Even *Salome* is marred by much unnecessary richness, as in Herod's speech: "I have jewels hidden in this place . . . a collar of pearls set in four rows. They are like unto moons chained with rays of silver. They are even as half a hundred moons caught in a golden net . . . I have amethysts of two kinds. . . . I have topazes yellow as are the eyes of tigers, and topazes that are pink . . . and green topazes. . . . I have opals. . . . I have onyxes like the eyeballs of a dead woman. I have moon stones . . . sapphires . . . chrysolites and beryls, and chrysoprases and rubies; I have sardonyx and hyacinth stones, and stones of chalcedony. . . ." Such richness of the jeweler's display is indeed as wearisome as that of a pedantic medieval *Lapidary*; and it now reminds one too much of Huysmans, whom Wilde was imitating, and of *Peter Whiffle*, that clearance-sale of all the curios that Carl Van Vechten had inherited from the "estates" of Wilde, Edgar Saltus and Ronald Firbank.

All that glitters in nature and life is not necessarily gold in art or poetry. We are not always dazzled by it as we read of it, we do not always see it as Cyril saw the hawk-faced gods. And Wilde's most poetic lies were often those that came most surprisingly, his most vivid and rich descriptions those of objects which had no insurance-value, his most poetic prose that which relied least on the prestige of Elizabethan poetry, of Biblical utterance or of the book-illustrator's art. In *The Young King*, Wilde himself reveals both the esthetic and the moral limitations of mere preciousness, and of the superficial beauty of jewels or brocades and riches which moth and rust corrupt. Brought up in Arcadian simplicity among the shepherds, the child of a morganatic royal marriage suddenly inherits the crown and discovers the splendors of a fabulous court; he becomes, at first, passionately addicted to the pursuit of all that glitters, till a series of dreams reveals to him the poverty and agony of the pearl-divers and weavers and other workers who toil to produce his lovely baubles. The young king then abandons these earthly splendors to pursue the absolute beauties of charity and saintliness. In *The Happy Prince*, Wilde had similarly hinted that the gold and jewels of the statue were less lovely than the charity and self-denial of the prince and the swallow; and in *The Nightingale and the Rose*, that the bird's self-sacrifice was at least as lovely as its song or as the rose that its blood had made red. But Wilde discovered in *The Young King* a new source of beauty, and his descriptions of the dismal attic where the weavers toil, a curious resurgence of an ancient Celtic myth of the other-world which had been handed down to Tennyson and the Pre-Raphaelites from such Arthurian romances as Chrétien de Troyes' *Ivain*, is at least as hallucinatingly vivid as Wilde's descriptions of more glittering beauties. In *The Birthday of the Infanta* too, the pathos of the hideous dwarf's love for the lovely royal child, and of his discovery of his own ugliness in the mirror, then of his broken-hearted death contrasted with the infanta's petulant annoyance at the loss of this human toy, all these are marred by no self-conscious humor or affectation of beauty; and the little monster's physical ugliness is as vividly depicted as that of a Velasquez dwarf, and indeed as poetic as the beautiful infanta's ugly insensitivity. With unerring strokes, Wilde here depicts rapidly, without stopping to moralize, to over-decorate or to entertain with unnecessary wit or humor.

In his later fables, Wilde thus rejected mere physical beauty in favor of a more transcendent beauty of art whose light shines forth from appearances often less glittering and sometimes even ugly. And he achieved his aim of dazzling not so much by the richness of what he described as by his way of describing it, by a kind of sublime that emanates, to a great extent, from the vivid description of contrasts, from a more firmly guided dialectic than that of the earlier tales, and from a greater unity of plot or singleness of purpose in the narrative's atmosphere. As a narrator, Wilde was less frequently tempted to err from his course through stagnant pools of description or wayward humor; and his atmosphere was at last perfectly suited to his plot, in an esthetic similar to that of the German *Maerchen*, of the macabre story or of the lyrical drama, where character development, by rooting the narrative too deep in the reality of verisimilitude, might mar the mythical reality of the unreal.

We cannot easily evaluate Wilde's techniques for attaining the sublime, or the theory that would justify them, without situating them first in a quest or controversy that has now lasted some two thousand

years. But our task allows little scope for a detailed historical survey of the
topic; and brevity soon suggests misleading generalizations, unless one is
careful to think in terms of the contexts of particular theories rather than
in terms of the theories themselves. Each theory of the sublime must thus
be viewed here as an attempt to organize and clarify the data and opinions
of its age and of a controversy the general problems of which determine
much of the theory's particular nature.

Most of the critics of antiquity, when they first examined poetry or
poetics, analyzed them dialectically, as Plato did, in terms of the known
values of another science, such as ethics or politics. But Aristotle's
formulation of analytical logic, the terms of which are applicable to all
sciences and belong to none, soon made it possible to determine rationally
the elements of poetry; and those of tragedy thus came to be defined in
Aristotle's *Poetics*. It was then found, however, that an unknown element
which escaped logical analysis yet remained to be defined. This element
was the sublime, whose existence and nature such critics as Longinus
determined intuitionally or psychologically, by observing in themselves or
in others the emotions that it aroused and by attempting to correlate these
with the passages of a poem that produced them. The element of the
sublime thus became the primary aim of many poets; but an emphasis on
the poem's educational effect on its audience led to a confusion between
oratory and poetry, which broadened the scope of a discussion that was
more and more devoted to morals or to rhetoric. Longinus, for instance,
identified the sublime, on the one hand, with the communication of the
poet's own moral virtues or those of his topic and, on the other hand,
with the rhetorical devices which allow art to imitate fitly the beauties of
nature, in fact to reproduce, for instance, in abrupt or disordered syntax,
the abruptness or disorder of the passions or the scene described. And
when Sir Joshua Reynolds, many centuries later, returned to a similar
discussion of the sublime in the art of painting, for which no rhetoric had
yet been formulated, he still reduced it so clearly to the depiction of moral
virtues that he preached little more than an art of illustrating noble rather
than merely elegant deportment.

By reducing to a limited number of theological mysteries all that
defied rational analysis, medieval scholasticism absorbed the sublime within
the miracles and confused the rest of poetics with rhetoric. Virgil thus
came to be variously revered, throughout the Middle Ages, as a prophet or
magician among rhetoricians or a pre-Christian saint; and apocalyptic
allegory became the aim of poets who, like Dante, hoped to transcend the
trivia of grammar, logic and rhetoric and attain the anagogical sublime.

The Humanists of the Renaissance again distinguished esthetics from theology, the esthetically miraculous from the theologically miraculous, the poet as creator of the beautiful from God as Creator of the Universe. They tended, however, especially Giangiorgio Trissino and Sperone Speroni, to think that a tragedy's audience could be moved to pity or fear only when its characters illustrated pity or fear; and this type of literal thinking led them also to identify the sublime with a poem's miraculous or marvelous content. Pagan myths and marvelous legends of chivalry, with their monsters and magicians, thus became favorite topics among such poets as Ariosto or Tasso; and the sublime, in the poetics of Tasso or Minturno, and later in the critical writings of Corneille, was variously identified with a magic which made the poet analogous to God, with the marvelous of profane legends or, if an ethical content were required, with the "merveilleux chrétien" of Tasso's epic, of Corneille's *Polyeucte* or of Milton's *Paradise Lost* as distinguished from the profane marvelous of Ariosto's epic, of *Le Cid* or of Spenser's *The Faerie Queen.*

But the sublime still seemed to elude all rational analysis; and gradually such critics as Gravina and Dubos returned to discussing it as an unknown quantity, a "je ne sais quoi," till the middle of the Eighteenth Century, while poets almost gave up all hope of attaining it, except by some chance felicity of sentiment or of wording. A new interest in epistemology, however, then revived discussions of the sublime, first in England and then in Germany, but with a new emphasis on taste and on the dimension from the work of art to its audience rather than from artists or subject-matter to work of art. Initiating this fruitful and more empiric or pragmatic type of investigation of the sublime, Edmund Burke made esthetics a study of the sensual and intellective rather than of the moral pleasures of art. And Hogarth suggested that the unknown quantity might reside in devices that do not follow known or rational canons of art, in the irregular rather than the regular, in the "clear serpentine line" and in sinuously indirect curves, in the winding streams of nature, for instance, rather than in the formally architectonic structures of the Palladian temples of art. If the analogy between geometry and logic were valid, this would mean that the poetic sublime resides in sinuously indirect statement rather than in direct proposition. In Germany, discussion of the beauties of non-classical masterpieces slowly led also to the formulation of various intuitional theories of judgment and of the sublime; and Romantic poets tended toward these views, at first, and developed a poetics of periphrasis and self-expression which allowed more scope for emotional or impassioned inspiration and, while stressing a renewed interest in the irrational and in the marvelous, generally preached what one might call a non-Euclidean conception of form.

The later Romantics, however, were not satisfied with these views. In an age of scientific experiment, of inventions and discoveries, they returned to a more exact and mechanistic conception of form and devised an inductive method which, positing the sublime as an actual infinite, worked toward it with the aid of techniques and devices which seemed likely to attain it. Such were, for instance, the experimental poetics of Poe, Baudelaire or Rimbaud; as magicians or hypnotists, in a curious mixture of scientific method and of the showmanship of the charlatan, these poets experimented on their readers with techniques of hallucination or obsession, with vividly objective description or hauntingly rhythmical repetition, the *diatyposis* and the *anaphora* which Longinus had recommended. And it was Oscar Wilde's distinction to be one of the first to apply these theories in English; but it was also his misfortune to achieve his ends more infrequently than Poe.

With his brashly American sense of expediency and showmanship, Poe had understood that his task demanded a total effort in which he could afford to despise no device, however trite or crude. Wilde was more fastidious and under-estimated the value of whole classes of devices which dazzle or deceive less sophisticated readers. In *The Canterville Ghost*, he could bring himself to use the conventionally melodramatic props of the macabre story only apologetically, with self-conscious humor; but Poe had used them without betraying any emotion that might weaken their effect. And in *The Picture of Dorian Gray*, Wilde avoided many of these props and substituted descriptions of rare and precious objects which demand of the reader more taste or learning and contribute little to the narrative's total atmosphere. In *The Sphinx*, whose apparition is so closely patterned on that of *The Raven*, Wilde likewise avoided the doggerel devices of obsessive rhythms and jingling rhymes which Poe had used so successfully. Wilde's failure to achieve his objective as often as Poe can thus be attributed, to a great extent, to his intellectual or esthetic prestige-needs and to inhibitions which prevented him from using some of the more crude or trite devices of his art. In his empirical quest of the sublime's actual infinite, Wilde had ignored whole categories of evidence, so that his inductive method was less reliable and his success less probable.

G. WILSON KNIGHT

Christ and Wilde

I do not claim to know the exact degree of Wilde's legal guilt. He himself said that "while there was much amongst the definite charges that was quite untrue" his life had certainly "been full of perverse pleasures" (De Profundis, The Works of Oscar Wilde, ed. G. F. Maine, 1948 etc.; 883). The nature of his relationship to his mother is said to have left him with what psychologists call a "mother-fixation" (Frank Brennard, Oscar Wilde, 1960; I. 15); the association recalls Byron's, though Byron's was less happy. His mother dressed him as a girl until he was nine (Brennard, I. 15). Like Byron, Wilde was a lover of children (Lord Byron: Christian Virtues, II. 75–83; Hesketh Pearson, The Life of Oscar Wilde, Penguin 1960 edn., XI. 187; XVII. 334), and both exerted a strong fascination over women. Both often appeared effeminate, and yet both were capable, when challenged, of disconcerting feats of male strength. Wilde's love of flowers and interest in both male and female dress—he started his literary career as editor of a woman's periodical— were allied with a robust physique, physical courage, intellectual brilliance and a devastating wit to give him a position of artistic and social domi- nance that proved intoxicating both to others and to himself. From youth onwards he maintained, like Byron, a boyish immaturity often difficult to distinguish from the integration of a seer.

Within was a strong idealism and a rich mine of human sympathy. His first play Vera or the Nihilists sets a justified revolution against a tyrannic aristocracy and touches solution under the crown—"this little fiery-coloured world" (IV)—an enlightened sovereign, and love; through these, unified and expanded, is glimpsed a solution to human misery. *Vera* is of a higher order than his subsequent dramas; it failed; but its key-thoughts continued to impregnate Wilde's serious writing. *The Soul of Man under Socialism* demonstrates the necessity of preserving the individual's freedom or soul-worth within our planning; seeing the royal, or aristo-cratic, valuations *as they exist in each one of us*, as sacred. The symbol of this soul-worth may be the crown; or more often riches, and especially jewels. Jewels and other rich solids constitute Wilde's central symbolism; for him the City of God is "like a perfect pearl" and "the pearl of my soul" a natural phrase (*De Profundis*; *Works*; 865, 866).

Throughout literature rich metals are used ambivalently. They may hold connotations of material greed or may be symbols of the transcen-dent. Jewels normally exert positive radiations. The Kingdom of Heaven is a "pearl" and the New Jerusalem made of precious stones (*Matthew*, XIII. 46; *Revelation*, XXI., 18–21). Dante's *Divina Commedia* sparkles, and Milton's *Paradise Lost* is loaded, with rich stones. We have Shakespeare's "mine eternal jewel" for the soul in *Macbeth* (III. i. 68), Othello's "pearl" as a love-symbol (V. ii. 346) and the jewel-imagery in *Pericles* (III. ii. 102; and see *The Shakespearian Tempest*, V. 222–3; also II. 65–9); Byron's contrast of "seraph"-eyed Aurora and Haidée in terms respectively of a jewel-like transcendence and flowery nature in *Don Juan* (XV. 45, 47, 58; XVI. 48); Yeats' metal-imagery and Gold Birds in *Sailing to Byzantium*; and the spiritualized gems at the conclusion of Sir Herbert Read's *The Green Child*. We may compare Charles Doughty's beautiful passage on gems in his *Travels in Arabia Deserta* (edn. of 1926; XI. 315): "Those indestructible elect bodies, as stars, shining to us out of the dim mass of matter, are comfortable to our fluxuous feeble souls and bodies; in this sense all gems are cordial and of an influence religious. These elemental flowering lights almost persuade us of a serene eternity." "Flowering"; and yet rich metals contrast with flowers in point of solidity. In them spirituality is solid and beauty permanent: even a miser's lust has a transcendental aspect.

Rich metals are apt correlatives to transcendence housed in male beauty. In the love-duologue of the *Song of Solomon* the female receives her best adulation in imagery of fertility (p. 212), the male in imagery of rich stones. His fingers are like "golden tapers" tipped with "topaz," his body "ivory" veined with "sapphire" and his limbs of "marble" and "gold" (V. 10–15). This supposedly physical description blends readily with a vision of the seraphic, as recorded by Daniel:

> . . . I saw a man standing, robed in linen, with a girdle of fine gold from Ophir round his waist, his body gleaming like a topaz, his face like

lightning, his eyes like lamps of fire, his arms and legs like the colour of burnished bronze, and the sound of his words like the noise of a crowd!

(*Daniel*, X. 5)

Such elaborated metallic associations would not be quite so suitable for a woman. We are reminded of the Oriental phrase "diamond body" (Norman O. Brown, noting Rilke's poetic quest for the hermaphroditic, *Life against Death*, 1959; XVI. 313), used to designate the etheric, or astral, body which interpenetrates and survives the physical.

Wilde as aesthete knew both the fascination and the danger of the transcendent housed in the material. Through young male beauty he saw an eternal, jewel-like, perfection. But his experience of it, as of rich stones too, was ambivalent, balanced between eye-lust and transcendence. Almost lust was transcendence; or rather the lust aroused was *a lust for the transcendent*. This was Wilde's star; it, like the Crown in *Vera*, should somehow, if joined to love, be the heart of a great good: a Christian good. The complexities are handled in his parables.

In *The Young King* a prince before his coronation dreams of those who suffer to make his luxury and state, and accordingly rejects his coronation finery for a beggar's clothes. Standing before the image of Christ he prays and is transfigured:

And lo! through the painted windows came the sunlight streaming upon him, and the sunbeams wove round him a tissued robe that was fairer than the robe that had been fashioned for his pleasure. The dead staff blossomed, and bare lilies that were whiter than pearls. The dry thorn blossomed, and bare roses that were redder than rubies. Whiter than fine pearls were the lilies, and their stems were of bright silver. Redder than male rubies were the roses, and their leaves were of beaten gold.

The flowering metals point a merging of nature into the transcendent. The "Glory of God" fills the church and as the Young King comes from the altar "no man dared look upon his face, for it was like the face of an angel."

Variations are played on the central theme. Our next hero, in *The Fisherman and his Soul*, gives up his soul, which henceforth exists without a "heart," for love of a Mermaid, the Soul returning to tempt him to crime with lures of gold and luxury. Here natural love and nature, with water and flowers as fertility symbols, are on the one side and the soul, crime, and riches are on the other. Riches, even when evil, are to be aligned with the "soul"—a key-concept in Wilde—here functioning as tempter. Easier alignments occur in *The Star-Child*, where a star-born child becomes a boy of beauty and Narcissistic pride, scorning poverty and ugliness and engaging in deliberate cruelty. Punished by the loss of his beauty and now himself an outcast, from the depths of his suffering he takes pity on a diseased begger; so winning back his beauty and being finally crowned as a king.

Wilde is trying to relate his central intuition of youthful beauty to love and good works. That a kind of love-wisdom rather than any normal love is his true centre can be seen indirectly from the contrast of a natural and flower-like love with the soul in *The Fisherman and his Soul*. Wilde senses a dangerous co-presence of selfishness and spirituality, an all-too-solid presence of a transcendency directly associated with the "soul," and yet seemingly as *infertile as rich gems*; and as dangerous. How, then, may the "soul" and its jewelled and seemingly infertile Eros be related to love and Christian values? Young royal figures help most, since their human beauty lives and acts within the temporal order under the Crown whose rich stones symbolize the eternal.

In *The Happy Prince* the aim is clearer: the parable expresses the potential sovereignty of youth-beauty or love-wisdom even though, in our era, it is constricted. The Happy Prince is a gilded city-statue with sapphires for eyes and a ruby on his sword-hilt, much admired for his beauty and like an "angel." He is a royal Eros. A Swallow, symbolizing the human self, leaves his lady, a Reed, because of her feminine ways, and rests beneath the statue, which is weeping for human misery. Being himself fixed, the Prince needs the Swallow for three missions, and sends him bearing his ruby and two sapphires in turn to a destitute mother and her fever-struck little boy; to a young author cold and starving; and to a little girl, seller of matches, in dire need. Finally he gets the Swallow to strip the gold-leaf from his body piece by piece to relieve the destitute within the city. The Happy Prince symbolizes *that within the erotic vision which is not being used*; recalling to our minds those stores of "hidden kindness and power" in a man of which Nietzsche speaks (*Thus Spake Zarathustra*, 55). Though set on high where he can *see* "all the ugliness" and "all the misery" of mankind, yet he himself "cannot move"; but though his heart is of "lead," his beauty has the needed wealth; and after he is melted down and only his leaden heart survives with the dead Swallow, God in his good time will welcome both to his 'garden of Paradise" and "city of gold." Every phrase is loaded. It is a consummate and final statement, even to the heart of lead. Though the emotion may be, or seem, worthless, it survives the fires of mortality.

The essence of love-wisdom is creativity. Plato's final doctrine in *The Symposium* defines it as the desire to "beget upon the thing of beauty"

(206); having glimpsed the transcendent and creative essence within the youth-bud more excelling than maturity, to make from this sight fine works in art or action (209). In two sonnets (113, 114; *The Mutual Flame*, I. v. 119–20) Shakespeare tells how the harmony seen in his Fair Youth is next seen everywhere, in all that is most deformed and ugly; Nietzsche speaks of "the creative friend that hath ever a perfect world in his gift" (*Thus Spake Zarathustra*, 16); and Robert Bridges of "our happiest earthly companionships" as holding a foretaste of (i) "salvation" and (ii) some "super-humanity" to be (*The Testament of Beauty*, IV. 1408–11). So too Christian love may be defined as the love "for the ideal of man in each individual" and to generate this love the admiration of *one* individual may be enough (Sir J. R. Seeley, *Ecce Homo*, 1865; XIV). Such is the doctrine within *The Happy Prince*: Eros, weeping for sympathy with human misery, wants the human soul to spend his wealth.

Difficulties remain. The beauty, unlike female beauty, is, as Shakespeare's Sonnets drive home (e.g. Sonnet 104), though a window into the eternal, yet in earthly terms transient; and so is the purity, or virtue, which it appears, for a while, to express. In *The Picture of Dorian Gray* the young hero of amazing beauty becomes, like the Star-Child, cruel and vicious, and though he remains outwardly young and perfect his advancing age and crimes are horribly objectified in the ever-changing and damning portrait, which recalls the externalized evil of *The Fisherman and his Soul*. What is the relation of human beauty to worth? Do we admire form and colour only, or do we in the act of adoration see through to the soul, as Spenser in his *Hymn in Honour of Beauty* (120–140) and *Epithalamion* (186) thought? Is human beauty simply in Byron's phrase "the precious porcelain of human clay"? Or shall we, looking inwards, compare it to "a lighted alabaster vase"? (*Don Juan*, IV. 11; VIII. 96). May not the soul-flame, when tested, prove ugly? Is there nothing both exquisite and permanent, except jewels, which are anyway infertile unless on a crowned king? *Dorian Gray* contains one of Wilde's finest passages on jewels (XI); and it is surely the subtlest critique of the Platonic Eros ever penned. Throughout Wilde's thought-adventures there is this analysis of the interrelationship of soul, beauty and Christian goodness. Somehow there must be a harmony and a permanence and a creative result. But how? Perhaps the truth can only be tragically defined; and perhaps, from the depths, he realized this.

Not only was Wilde's a quest of a high order, but it had strong Christ-like affinities. The New Testament wavelength and Biblical style of the Parables is obvious; and from his youth onwards Wilde was deeply attracted, and in his works again and again engaged, by the Christian religion. In *Salome* a decadent and bejewelled paganism in a sulphurous atmosphere of beauty and blood-lust asserts itself statically and repetitively against the equally repetitive denunciations of Jokanaan, or John the Baptist, whom Salome desires. Always in Wilde the two worlds want to meet. Here they co-exist in unhealthy opposition: the atmosphere is like pressure before thunder.

We must see Wilde's homosexual engagements in the context of these works. They were prompted by his innate love of all youth from children upwards and also by his own state of male-female, and often seemingly boy-like, integration. The drama of his relationship to Lord Alfred Douglas, with its see-saw of idealisms and angers, repeats the story of those Sonnets of Shakespeare of which Wilde has himself left us a study in *The Portrait of Mr. W. H.*, relating the Fair Youth to the boy-girl actors of Shakespeare's stage. Wilde's less idealistic engagements were prompted by (i) the instinct, as felt by Shakespeare, Byron and Nietzsche, to plunge low when the disparity between the near-integrated self and the community becomes unbearable . . . so that we find him writing, "Tired of being on the heights, I deliberately went to the depths in the search for new sensation" (*De Profundis; Works*, 857); and (ii) by a genuine liking for the lower orders of society; not any deep and lasting love for any one person, but a lightning contact with thrill in the very disparity and sexual ratification of human unity. He once said that he found the young men of the underworld as dangerously fascinating as "panthers" (*De Profundis; Works*, 882).

And because there is an exhibitionist compulsion on such men to reveal themselves, Wilde could not remain content with his social mask. Though he was genuinely fascinated by the glitter of high society which was, like his jewels, a symbol of his aim, he also saw through the superficiality, making his terms with it, like Hamlet and Byron, by wit. That could not last; his scornful speech of congratulation to his first-night audience for admiring one of his comedies was in part genuine, the more so since he must have known that the play was inadequate. So, as though compelled by an instinct for self-revelation, he half-willingly exposed his life to society's revulsion. He played with fire, "with that tiger, Life" (Pearson, XIV. 255), in deadly earnest, and when he might have done so refused, again and again, to escape the conflagration. "That," he said, "would be a backward step" (Pearson, XV. 276). This does not mean that he did not suffer, but simply that he was impelled from the depths to put in train and abide by a sequence of events which would lead to suffering. As Lewis Broad puts it, "the vision of St. Sebastian, 'the youngest of the martyrs,' had vividly impressed him, years before" (*The Truth about Oscar*

Wilde; 1957 edn.; XV. 175). Such men may appear to embrace their martyrdom—"I had to pass on" (*De Profundis*; *Works*, 866)—but it remains a martyrdom, a crucifixion, a self-exhibition in agony and shame. The shame may be of the essence; at the least it shatters all the pseudo-dignities and masks of our lying civilization.

At his trial Wilde also lied in answer, though he might have done better to speak out. And yet he did, on the important issue, speak firmly. The famous letter of his to Lord Alfred Douglas containing the phrase "your slim-gilt soul that walks between passion and poetry" may appear over-decorative, but the words are precise. "Slim-gilt," if we remember *The Happy Prince*, Wilde's jewel-symbolism and the term "diamond body" for the etheric or spirit body interpenetrating the physical . . . , is an exact term for the seraphic intuition. "Between passion and poetry" matches the blend of instinct and intellect within the Platonic Eros. Of this blend Lord Alfred Douglas had been the symbol, the living truth. Faced with this letter and the words in Lord Alfred's sonnet on "the love that dare not speak its name," Wilde replied:

> The "love that dare not speak its name" in this century is such a great affection of an elder for a younger man as there was between David and Jonathan, such as Plato made the very basis of his philosophy, and such as you find in the sonnets of Michelangelo and Shakespeare.

He continued by asserting its "spiritual" nature and its relation to "works of art"; its worth as "the noblest form of affection"; its natural quality and its intellectual status. According to Lewis Broad this defence has been called "the finest speech of an accused man since that of Paul before Agrippa" (Broad, XIV. 167; *Acts*, XXVI).

Wilde's *De Profundis*, written from prison, is a commentary, from a Nietzschean standpoint, on his tragic experience. Sorrow and suffering are now experienced as revelations of the creative purpose; the wholeness of his own drama is accepted and ratified; the deep insights of his parables, which he recalls, are lived. There is no repentance, no morality in any usual sense, but there is a lengthy and profound concentration on Christ. From the start Christian sympathies had run concurrently with his Hellenic and aesthetic passions. Now Christ is his central interest. He is seen as, above all, the supreme artist; more, as the first and greatest romantic, behind the romances of medievalism, of Shakespeare, and of more modern times. He notes his respect, so like Wilde's own—as indeed he himself says (*De Profundis*; *Works*; 875)—for children as exemplars for us all; and his insistence on wholeness, recalling how he himself had written in *The Soul of Man under Socialism* "that he who would lead a Christ-like life must be entirely and absolutely himself" (*Works*, 867). Christ had a strange sympathy with sinners:

> The world had always loved the saint as being the nearest possible approach to the perfection of God. Christ, through some divine instinct in him, seems to have always loved the sinner as being the nearest possible approach to the perfection of man . . . To turn an interesting thief into a tedious honest man was not his aim . . . The conversion of a publican into a Pharisee would not have seemed to him a great achievement. But in a manner not yet understood of the world he regarded sin and suffering as being in themselves beautiful holy things and modes of perfection.
>
> (*Works*, 877)

Wilde admits the danger, and also agrees on the need for some kind of repentance, viewed in Shakespearian wise (*The Sovereign Flower*, V. 249) simply as *recognition*, in order to harmonize and ratify the whole (877–8). He is trying to see life-as-art, with tragic form. More precisely, he is asserting, in the manner of Browning's *The Statue and the Bust*, that within the criminal there may exist certain elements of fire and courage necessary to perfection but too often absent from morality. He is thinking less of any sin of his own—he himself regrets nothing (866)—than of the fascination exerted on him by the young "panthers" and "gilded snakes," whose "poison was part of their perfection" (882), of the underworld. His main emphasis on Christ's repudiation of legality and hypocrisy is valid, and his relation of Christ's Judaea to his own Britain (876) reasonable. The essay is written from a Nietzschean standpoint recognizing that "between the famous and the infamous there is but one step, if as much as one" (862).

　　Christ is a key to Wilde's life. I quote again from Hesketh Pearson. Wilde was "drawn to the personality of Jesus Christ" (XI. 188) and his interest "increased every year until at length he almost identified himself with Christ and often spoke in parables" (X. 141). "Both thought and taught in stories, and both had a strong intuition of their tragic destiny" (XIII. 218). One of his parables, *The Doer of Good*, was on Christ (XIII. 218; *Works*, 843). "He saw himself in the role of Christ, the shouts of his first-night audiences being his hosannas," with Calvary to follow (XV. 282). He felt that his life needed a tragic completion (XV. 282) and wooed disaster "under the influence of a mystical concept" (XV. 284). While there was still time to flee, "He has resolved," said his brother, "to stay, to face it out, to stand the music like Christ" (XV. 301). Finally "his own condemnation and sufferings had completed the parallel with Jesus which for many years he had instinctively drawn" (XVI. 323); and "in his last years the two figures whom Wilde was readiest to talk about were Napoleon and Jesus Christ" (XVIII. 358).

Those who knew Wilde personally recognized a stature impossible to recapture from reported epigram and printed essay. Beerbohm Tree's comment is typical: "Oscar was the greatest man I have ever known—and the greatest gentleman" (Pearson, XIV. 232). His record of lived virtue recalls Byron's, though he lacked Byron's thrust and range of purpose. The softer intuitions of both were on the wavelength of Christ's. Resemblances to Christ are clear in Wilde's Byronic love of children, his egotism blended with humility, his repartee, his utter lack of malice, his forgiveness and Timonlike generosity (e.g. Pearson, XVII. 335); his magnanimity, his refusal to save himself, and patient endurance of shame. His record of kindly actions is as high as Byron's (e.g. Pearson, V. 65; VI. 73); his fight for removing the hideous wrongs of children in prison alone (*Letter to the Daily Chronicle, Works*; 897–903), when set against the system, leaves no question as to Wilde's moral superiority over the society that condemned him. Long before his own fall, he had like Christ a natural sympathy with all outcasts (Pearson, VII. 93–4). His natural friendliness for the rough and low from his American tour onwards is recorded again and again. Active criminals were rapidly deflected by his courteous and kindly reception (Pearson, XV. 273; XVIII. 367) and what he wrote of Christ was true of himself: "He does not really teach one anything, but by being brought into his presence one becomes something" (*De Profundis; Works*, 878). Naturally, he made friends in prison. A warder, named Martin, at Reading gaol wrote of him: "What that poet was before he went to prison I care not. What he may have been after he left prison I know not. One thing I know, however, that while in prison he lived the life of a saint, or as near that holy state as poor mortal can ever hope to attain" (Broad, XVII. 193). Vincent O'Sullivan received the same impression: "If terrible sufferings courageously borne, the enduring of dire injustice and reviling without complaint, be matter of saintliness, then Wilde was a saint" (Pearson, XVIII. 358).

How far the analogy to Christ is valid we cannot say without a much deeper knowledge of the forces in play than we at present possess; and it would be wise to suspend judgement. Honesty at least will not deny that it would have been our loss had Wilde's life been other than it was. This is not to say that his actions were right, but rather that to us his actions together with their consequences are extraordinarily valuable; they are at least tragically justified. His story dramatizes much that lies close to the essence of art. His statement that "the artist must live the complete life, must accept it as it comes and stands like an angel before him, with its drawn and two-edged sword" (Pearson, XVIII. 357)—"angel" to match the homosexual-seraphic and "two-edged" to cover tragedy—is *not* true of the artist; but it may be true of those who attempt the yet higher and far more difficult quest of living their art. Wilde's most famous works were written for money, and are of the second order only; and his paradoxes, on paper, pall. His genius went into his life, his living talk; into his spoken or written parables; and into *Dorian Gray*, itself an extended parable. He was by instinct a teacher. When his last days are called "unproductive," Hesketh Pearson justly comments, "Yet no one has ever called Christ or Socrates unproductive because each of these spoke his thoughts instead of writing them down" (XVIII. 366); and each, like Wilde, uncomplainingly paid the penalty demanded by civilization for their impact.

Wilde's life is a drama, and seen in all its excess, its brilliance, its degradation and its tragedy, it has the form needed to correspond to the matters contained. His flamboyance, exhibitionism and heady enjoyment of success, these must be admitted; and also his shocking inability—Timon-like in this as in his generosity—to handle money (Pearson, XVIII. 363), his dishonest misleading of his legal helpers, and his unjust attack on Lord Alfred Douglas written from prison. But all must be judged in relation to the difficulties inherent in his life's central, Blakean, aim: to make of the senses elements of a new spirituality, to cure the soul by the senses and the senses by the soul (*The Picture of Dorian Gray*, II; *Works*, 29, 31). This aim he carried through with a daring consistency; it motivated alike his aestheticism, his anti-social acts and his perception of Christ. About his lowest engagements there was an element of the sacramental. Of cruelty he knew as little as he knew of caution; his instincts were of a childlike, positive and embracing kind. In these terms he lived and acted in allegiance to the royalty of the crowned and diamonded Eros. His sin was total self-expression acted out in spontaneity "not wisely but too well"; and he took tragedy uncomplainingly in his stride.

His influence for good, though it was an influence that cold print cannot record, was empowered by a Falstaffian and Byronic humour (e.g. Pearson, quoting Douglas, XVIII. 359; also 367). According to *Thus Spake Zarathustra* our new, Renaissance, way beyond religion must include humour, without which "truth" is suspect (56), for "all good things laugh" (73). "I have hallowed laughter" (73) means the hallowing of much before which religion veils its eyes. Powys in *Rabelais* (1948; Part IV) explains this new life-wisdom. Wilde went far to incarnate it.

EPIFANIO SAN JUAN, JR.

The Action of the Comedies

Aside from the meaningful attempts at romantic drama in the late eighties, Wilde's dramatic achievement consists of the four social comedies which occupied him from 1892, when *Lady Windermere's Fan* appeared, to 1895, when *The Importance of Being Earnest* was staged with resounding success. During this period the "domestic" comedies of Henry Arthur Jones and the "problem plays" of Arthur Wing Pinero flourished; pieces like *The Second Mrs. Tanqueray* (1894) or *The Case of Rebellious Susan* (1894) confirmed certain fashions in playmaking. To a great extent they helped establish the taste for the mannered gesture and the emphatic projection of social attitudes in the plays. Such trends, including analogous tendencies in dramatic acting, were ushered in when the audience, composed largely of the middle class, replaced the social "elite" as theatrical arbiters. What the middle class demanded, the playwrights and actors generally gave: melodramatic plots to excite the passions. Meanwhile, the actors attuned their methods to the unsophisticated mentality of the audience, heightening emotional virtuosity and dispensing altogether with the neoclassical stylized and formal manner of the preceding century.

In the nineteenth century, Scribe and Sardou introduced the vogue of the "well-made" play on the European as well as on the English stage. The ingenious construction of their plots and the artificial techniques and devices they exploited to increase suspense easily appealed to the masses. For the sake of a sensational twist or a climactic scene, playwrights of this school subordinated character, dialogue, and all other elements to the aim of producing an immediate effect on the spectators.

Wilde's comedies embody the melodramatic and farcical strains of the fashionable, "well-made" play—but with a difference. Commentators have noticed in his plays the disparity between speech and action, the disharmony between the conventional action and the unconventional characters and their speeches. For instance, while the aristocrats generally heed formal propriety, the radical sympathies of Lord Darlington or Lord Illingworth wreak havoc on propriety and every genteel orthodoxy. Within the framework of the conventional and credible plot, there exists a steady iconoclastic current of conversation. This yields intellectual farce which bears no reformatory purpose or ideal except the catharsis aroused by the dialectics of irony and sophistry. One can perceive in this kind of comedy a link between the "perverted grotesqueness" of the Savoy operas and the rational bourgeois-baiting of Shaw.

The delightful make-believe that is the substance of Wilde's comedies draws strength chiefly from the effervescent wit and the mental alertness that inform the dialogue. This is conveyed by the easy, graceful prose. The idiom Wilde assigns to his characters, though often out of character, serves as a versatile instrument both for simple fun and serious mockery. Perhaps Wilde was just too clever and smart in the exercise of his histrionic power; he exhibits too "wildly" his penchant for "posing." How far has he really gone toward achieving a new dramatic form? One recalls that he began his career with imitations: *Vera* and *The Duchess of Padua*. There one notes the violent peripeteia, the "strong" curtains, and the sudden conversions or changes of heart of the leading characters. But in the witticisms of the villains these plays foreshadow the concentrated and ingenious paradoxes already marked in *A Florentine Tragedy* and in *Salome*, despite their emotionalism. This verbal wit culminates in the mathematical finesse with which maxims and epigrams are lined up in smooth sequence; witness the exchanges of the dandies in Lord Darlington's room in *Lady Windermere's Fan*.

With the comedies, Wilde modifies the "thesis" element of the "well-made" play by blending serious and trivial implications into a composite whole. Two temperaments or dispositions—one involving aggressive, worldly cynicism with its detached sensitivity and the other involving primitive emotionalism—clash in crucial scenes. One observes how the dandies counteract the propensity to mawkishness which continually mars the plays of Augier and Dumas *fils*. In *The Importance of Being Earnest*, serious meanings are conveyed by stylized language which, however, tends to slow down the movement of the plot. This feature has led many critics to formulate the notion of an inherent incongruity in the form of Wilde's comedies. For example, one reads the notion of a "divided self," a hypothesis that exists only when the reader isolates certain contradictions apart from the other elements that constitute the play's total pattern of meaning.

Critics have remarked that between the sentimental plots of the comedies, where passion and seriousness predominate, and the dandiacal world of the villains, there exists an irreconcilable difference. Wilde's philistine self supposedly begs pardon from society for his excesses when we see, for example, Lord Illingworth pleading to Mrs. Arbuthnot on behalf of his illegitimate son. Meanwhile, his dandiacal self continues to defy that society and to proclaim absolute freedom so that he can express his own personal tastes and values. Torn between his contempt for empty social values and his desire to be accepted and praised by society, Wilde is supposed to have created plays in which the issues and problems are illogically posed and left unsolved or unresolved. For example, Arthur Ganz, in exploring this idea of Wilde's "divided self" (better, split sympathies), contends that Wilde "could not write as the ordinary satirist does, for where the satirist admires a social norm and ridicules deviations from it, the Wildean dandy is himself a deviation and ridicules the social norm." The only form of a resolution in the plays can be found in the dandiacal joke, where external and formal manners triumph over internal moods and morals.

Censure has been levelled too against the dandy as an "idealized image"—a caricature or dummy. Other personages in the comedies impress the reader as being flat cardboard surfaces. But, Wilde himself retorts, is the dandy's image of lower value than the "round" lifelike creations of the realists? When a critic accused Ben Jonson's characters of being masks and ready-made counters, Wilde countered by arguing that ready-made personages—like Iago or Sir Andrew Aguecheck—are "not necessarily either mechanical or wooden." He urges us, in other words, to accept the character of a particular person in the play as a *donnée* which the play seeks to render in concrete terms. Jonson's comic personages are not abstractions but types. The dramatist can use, instead of psychological analysis, a more dramatic and direct method, namely, "mere presentation." In any case Wilde ascribes to Jonson the importance of having introduced "formal research" into the "laws of expression and composition," embodying in himself "the most concentrated realism with encyclopaedic erudition." His comedies intermingled London slang and learned scholarship, his classical lore giving "flesh and blood to his characters." Hence Jonson's "incongruity" Wilde finds congenial.

Now one fundamental premise of comedy is that man, being finite, does not know all the situations that affect his life. His knowledge, far from being complete, is wavering and uncertain; he has many "blind spots." By reason of his limitations in time and space, man is barred from knowing many of the factors and forces that will affect his fate. This is perhaps why a more or less rigid classification of characters exists in the comedies; for in man's tendency to justify himself and his importance, he becomes obsessed with a certain quality or attitude. Eventually one can identify these obsessed figures with fixed patterns of action and response.

We have in Wilde's comedies, for example, the woman with the past: Mrs. Erlynne and Mrs. Arbuthnot. On the other hand, Sir Robert Chiltern and Jack Worthing nourish a past which later comes to affect their lives by some twist of circumstance, by some inscrutable concourse of events. Both sets of characters realize their true identity, in a sense, by sharing the knowledge of their past with other people. Counterposed to these "guilty" personages is the judicial role of the strict Puritan obsessed with categorical "good" and "evil": witness Lady Windermere, Hester Worsley, Lady Chiltern. Lady Bracknell, in this group, stands out by reason of her "dandiacal" or witty predilections. It will be seen that Lady Bracknell's spontaneous caprice of taste and judgment is closely related to the behavior of the dandies Jack and Algernon; the wit of these two "clowns" permeates the atmosphere of the play, and vitalizes the stratified and highly symmetrical society they live in. The vitalizing element stems from the almost animal exuberance with which they translate preposterous ideas into action; as when both of them engage in "Bunburying," sharing the disguise of "Ernest."

Wilde's ironic wit has usually been regarded as antithetical to the moral questions and issues that he treats in the action of the play. Actually the total impression the comedies give is that of an integration of opposing viewpoints. It is as if a *discordia concors* has been attained in the structure of the plays. One example of this integration or combining of contraries is the reduction of manners to a game the moment the manners that form public conduct are subject to analysis. The comedies reveal the play-element at work in social affairs. They suggest that other forces, chiefly the instinctive and the irrational, exert a decisive influence on human behavior. Johan Huizinga's insight into the play-element in civilization is relevant here: "Play only becomes possible . . . when an influx of *mind* breaks down the absolute determinism of the cosmos. The very existence of play continually confirms the supra-logical nature of the human situation." The impulse of "play" works also in the manipulation of the dialogue. The dynamism of the verbal activity helps to liberate obsessed minds from peculiarities that the laws and taboos of customary intercourse have brought about. Dialogue stirs thought, and thought opens up possibilities of human growth.

Another aspect that one should bear in mind is the inter-relation between character and situation in the comedies. In Wilde's poetic dramas, the protagonists tend to acquire tragic magnitude as the plot grows complicated to the point where it challenges the protagonists to act in such a way that they reveal the sublime forces working through them. The heroic self looms large in *Salome*, where the action springs from Salome's obsession, Salome being alternately drawn to, and repelled by, Jokannan. Wilde himself locates the tragic quality in character, the comic in situation; thus the comedies exploit "strong" curtains, build-up of suspense, and radical transpositions of thought and impressions. The manipulation of situations follows from the given premises which the exposition of the first act makes clear, allowing development only in certain directions. Often the action falls within a schematic frame which approximates a game. Accordingly *The Importance of Being Earnest* has been described as "a reserved and stylized sybaritic dance." One critic has demonstrated the elaborate courtship dance in the second half of Act II and the first scene of Act III, when the couples unite and separate again. This systematic movement forms part of the symmetry of situation and dialogue that organizes the whole play. Not only does this visual choreography discipline the violence of farce by creating "aesthetic distance," but it also protects the drama from the realistic judgment that it is, in the pejorative sense, "contrived."

Wilde's most significant achievement is that he successfully combined the would-be serious subject, which often verges on sentimentality, with gay verbal wit and paradox. Situations that would otherwise be unreasonably pathetic—the comedies have strong affinities with popular extravaganza and melodrama—are sustained by the intellectual energy of the dialogue. Wilde exploits artificiality for jesting purposes, as in *The Importance of Being Earnest*; yet, amidst the absurdity of behavior, we hear the delicately pointed barbs of social criticism. Disguised within seemingly irresponsible quips are seriously thought-out comments on a variety of subjects.

Most critics of Wilde's plays, concentrating more on the humorous context than on the particularities of speech and thought, have dismissed the continuities of sense in the individual epigrams. There need be no qualms in taking the aphorisms at their conceptual level, despite the hilarious joke that threatens to explode them. Although Wilde repeatedly erects sensible propositions only to refute them, the propositions nonetheless remain valid reasoning. Just as Byron, in *Don Juan*, demonstrates to the full his talent for "nihilstic" humor, so Wilde does the same in the comedies. And just as Byron presents valid caricatures of vices and foibles of the Regency period, so Wilde articulates, in ironic modes, his condemnation of the follies of "decadent" society in the late nineteenth century.

I now aim to interpret in each play the witty utterances and their ironic qualifications with the purpose of tracing the action, that is, the continuity of meaning and wholeness of thematic pattern. To apprehend the distinctive qualities of Wilde's satire, one must go beyond plot and character and attend also to the verbal texture and the correspondence of speech with character, plot, and theme.

The satire of the comedies does not so much lie in plot or character as in language, its imagery and its connotations, the dialogue being a "running accompaniment" to the visible physical performance. According to Eric Bentley, Wilde's "dialogue, which sustains the plot, or is sustained by it, is an unbroken stream of comment on all the themes of life which the plot is so far from broaching. . . . Wildean 'comment' is a pseudo-irresponsible jabbing at all the great problems, and we would be justified in removing the prefix 'pseudo' if the Wildean satire, for all its naughtiness, had not a cumulative effect and a paradoxical one. Flippancies repeated, developed, and, so to say, elaborated almost into a system amount to something in the end—and thereby cease to be flippant. What begins as a prank ends as a criticism of life."

Wilde's subtle and delicate witticisms, then, are not comic but "serious relief." Although he has no serious plot and no really credible character, Wilde achieves a peculiar effect in counterpointing agile criticism with the absurdities of action. Thus one can hardly catch his "philosophy" in order to approve or denounce it. The irony involves the contrast between "the elegance and savoir-faire of the actors and the absurdity of what they actually do." This contrast, integral to the plays, is Wilde's efficient vantage point for ridiculing the aristocracy. The aristocrat's smooth, solid appearance, reflecting inner emptiness, is matched by the inversions of standards so as to disclose what these standards really mean: earnestness is equated with false seriousness, priggishness with hypocrisy, etc. With Congreve, Meredith, and Shaw, Wilde holds that the ironic attitude to life sees more than the deceptive, trivial surface that everyday reality confronts us with.

"LADY WINDERMERE'S FAN"

Wilde's first comedy *Lady Windermere's Fan* was written in 1891 and produced at the St. James' Theatre on February 20, 1892. The difficulty Wilde experienced in its composition centers on the fact that he could not "get a grip of the play"; he confesses, "I can't get my people real." To dispel any wrong impression about the play's "form and spirit," Wilde himself delineates the action thus:

> The psychological idea that suggested to me the play is this. A woman who has had a child, but never known the passion of maternity (there are such women), suddenly sees the child she has abandoned falling over a precipice. There wakes in her the maternal feeling—the most terrible of all emotions—a thing that weak animals and little birds possess. She rushes to rescue, sacrifices herself, does follies—and the next day she feels "This passion is too terrible. It wrecks my life. I don't want to be a mother any more." And so the fourth act is to me the psychological act, the act that is newest, most true. For which reason, I suppose, the critics say "There is no necessity for Act IV." But the critics are of no importance. They lack instinct. They have not the sense of Art.

Notice how Wilde isolates the maternal response of Mrs. Erlynne in Act III, when she pursues Lady Windermere to Lord Darlington's room and then anxiously but successfully persuades her daughter to return to her husband at the risk of being caught in a shameless act. Mrs. Erlynne, compelled by a natural instinct shared by "weak animals," performs a sacrifice which requires utter selflessness. She forgets her worldly ambitions; she affirms the truth and integrity of human affections. When she reflects on her action, she begins to understand that all her life she has been preparing for that "climax," that crucible of her life. The crisis displayed her innate love for her daughter, her instinctive care for her happiness.

When Lord Windermere inquires about the purpose of her visit in Act IV, Mrs. Erlynne replies with "serious voice and manner." Her voice has an accent suffused with "a note of deep tragedy." For this moment "she reveals herself." She intends no "pathetic scene" with her daughter. She reassures him: "I have no ambition to play the part of a mother. Only once in my life have I known a mother's feelings. That was last night. They were terrible—they made me suffer—they made me suffer too much. For twenty years, as you say, I have lived childless—I want to live childless still." But though she might want "to live childless," she nonetheless has proven herself a genuine mother in feeling. She has shown at least that potency for losing herself, that selfless love, dramatized in an episode which exactly reproduces what she herself has done. This time she can predict the consequence: exactly what has happened to her. With full consciousness she directs her daughter's fate, as though she had never abandoned her. She thus aborts the near "repetition" of her life; now the daughter can live with a memory of this experience and hopefully be the wiser for it.

What Mrs. Erlynne doesn't know is that the passionate impulse and energy that drove her to abandon her child and husband for an illicit passion presuppose the same warmth and impulsive selflessness that she exhibits in Lord Darlington's room in trying to save her child from dishonor. She disregards the possibility that Lord Augustus might refuse her afterwards; her sole concern is for the untarnished reputation of her daughter. Had she been more egoistic and calculating, she could not have easily accepted the "scapegoat" function she assumed at the moment of crisis. But being an impetuous person whose emotion of love can truly possess her—it was not her fault that her lover deserted her, she claims— she acts in unconscious obedience to her real, maternal nature. Has she changed since her disgrace? Scarcely. She is as warm, alive, and—except for her shrewdness and firm, alert intelligence—as exuberant as before.

So Mrs. Erlynne declares she has no "ambition to play" the mother's part, having played it a while ago in Lord Darlington's room. The fact is that she no longer has any need to pose or play the role of mother to Lady Windermere; she has acted in consonance with her maternal nature, sincere and faithful to herself. She has revealed herself as a mother against her social instinct for mere pretense. She herself thought she was heartless—an illusion dispelled in Act IV when she cries out: "I thought I had no heart; I find I have, and a heart doesn't suit me. . . . Somehow it doesn't go with modern dress. It makes one look old. And it spoils one's career at critical moments."

In the society of the Windermeres, to have a "heart" goes against the grain of characters like the Duchess of Berwick, Mr. Dumby, Mr. Cecil Graham, Lord Augustus Lorton, and their motley group. In society, fashion rules. Why, indeed, should men care for "purity and innocence," Cecil Graham remarks; "A carefully thought-out buttonhole is much more effective." Appearance governs norms; Mrs. Erlynne says: "Repentance is quite out of date. And besides, if a woman really repents, she has to go to a bad dressmaker, otherwise no one believes in her." The portrait of herself in her youth shows her "dark hair" and her "innocent expression" supposed to be "in fashion" then. In the ballroom full of "palms, flowers, and brilliant lights," the names of guests serve as the tokens or counters of a game where empty frivolity occupies everyone. Lord Darlington refers to Lady Windermere as "the mask of his real life, the cloak to hide his secret," with respect to her husband's secret.

Wilde presents the question of true identity in all his comedies. Who am I?—that is, how define the network of social relations that condition and ultimately determine my public image? How articulate the stream of consciousness, impulses, feelings, and intuitions whose center I am? In Act I, the figure of Mrs. Erlynne denotes simply a woman of "more than doubtful character," casually mentioned by the gallants and dowagers; before the curtain falls, Lord Windermere exclaims, "I dare not tell her who this woman really is," after his wife's rebuke. We catch also the name of Mr. Hopper in an early scene, but Mr. Hopper is a puppet who offers a relief by contrast. While he is identified with "Australia" and "kangaroos," Mrs. Erlynne's presence begins to establish the profound emotional relationships in the play which are later to be clarified.

Quite obviously Mrs. Erlynne wears the trappings of a mysterious character. Lady Windermere, in Act III, disdainfully asks, "What have I to do with you?" to which she replies humbly, "Nothing." To Lord Windermere she is, in Act IV, "a divorced woman going about under an assumed name, a bad woman preying upon life." By the end of Act IV, Mrs. Erlynne acquires the attributes of being "very clever" and "very good." She progresses from anonymous tormentor of the Windermeres to a congenial "matron" of society. The development of the play as a whole involves the gradual clarification of her identity. Bit by bit human relations are particularized and objectified in action. If this process depicts the complexities of human nature, it also exposes the hollowness of social relations. As Lord Augustus, intrigued by Mrs. Erlynne's identity, puts it: "None of us men do look what we really are. Demmed good thing, too. What I want to know is this. Who is she? Where does she come from? Why hasn't she got any demmed relations? Demmed nuisance, relations! But they make one so demmed respectable." He expresses the point of the drama accurately in that human relationships give persons an identity, even a distinctive "humor." Whereas Mrs. Erlynne, despite the "curse" of her past, affirms the sanctity of the Windermeres' marriage and in fact condemns herself for violating orthodox morality, the dandies affirm the value of their anarchic views on marriage. To Lady Plymdale, Mrs. Erlynne and her ilk are aids to her flirtations:

LADY PLYMDALE: . . . I assure you, women of that kind are most useful.
    They form the basis of other people's marriages.
DUMBY: What a mystery you are!
LADY PLYMDALE: (Looking at him) I wish you were!
DUMBY: I am—to myself. I am the only person in the world I should like
    to know thoroughly. . . .

The knowledge of self as well as of other people serves as the focal interest here. It is the theme which underlies the movement of the plot; complication, crisis, and resolution are all oriented toward revealing the actual personalities behind the masks of the *dramatis personae* who initiate the conflict, or comment on it.

The best way to explain how the matter of true identity and knowledge of self is concretely rendered in the play is to dwell on certain motifs that coalesce into what may properly be termed a symbolic cluster. In Act I we hear this dialogue:

> LADY WINDERMERE: Well, you kept paying me elaborate compliments the whole evening.
>
> LORD DARLINGTON: (smiling). Ah, now-a-days we are all of us so hard up, that the only pleasant things to pay are compliments. They're the only thing we can pay.

Lady Windermere accuses him of saying "a whole heap of things that he doesn't mean," to which he retorts: "Ah, but I did mean them."

Wilde deftly foregrounds the buried image in "paying," and puns on the "paying" of debts and compliments. We see Lady Windermere asserting her right as wife to peep into her husband's bank account. She observes that "now-a-days people seem to look on life as a speculation." Lord Darlington says in this vein that most women "now-a-days, are rather mercenary." Likewise Dumby remarks casually, "Awfully commercial women now-a-days." All these allusions to "buying" and "selling" converge in Lady Windermere's accusation that Mrs. Erlynne belongs to that class who "are bought and sold." This charge brings up the idea of Mrs. Erlynne's spiritual struggles: while she tries to "buy" her way into society, she is at the same time "paying" for it by blackmailing Lord Windermere. In effect she is capitalizing on that sordid past for which she has been ostracized. She says to her daughter, "One pays for one's sin, and then one pays again, and all one's life one pays." Meanwhile the Duchess of Berwick registers the impression that Mrs. Erlynne is a wealthy woman, whereas we know that she receives blackmail money from her son-in-law; Lord Windermere pays for the honor of his house. The Duchess, on her part, knows the "value" of Mr. Hopper for the stupid Agatha.

But the most significant context in which the question of actual value occurs is in Act II, when Mrs. Erlynne urges Lord Windermere to bestow on her a "fictitous inheritance" so as to facilitate her marriage with Lord Augustus. She says to him: "It would be an additional attraction, wouldn't it? You have a delightful opportunity of paying me a compliment, Windermere. But you are not very clever at paying compliments. I am afraid Margaret doesn't encourage you in that excellent habit. It's a great mistake on her part. When men give up saying what is charming, they give up thinking what is charming." Set against Lord Darlington's compliments, Lord Windermere's signify the price one pays for social acceptance. Mrs. Erlynne needs the money to get back into society's fold.

When Lady Windermere, in the last act, decides to confess her folly to her husband, her mother dissuades her:

MRS. ERLYNNE: . . . You say you owe me something?
LADY WINDERMERE: I owe you everything.
MRS. ERLYNNE: Then pay your debt by silence. That is the only way in which it can be paid.

Mrs. Erlynne's investment "pays off" here. She has exercised her will on her daughter; she has shown "devotion, unselfishness, sacrifice." She has fulfilled what she felt before, when she was challenged by the situation: "What can I do? I feel a passion awakening within me that I never felt before. What can it mean? The daughter must not be like the mother—that would be terrible. How can I save her?"

Fearing a repetition of the past, Mrs. Erlynne strives for dynamic growth and the enhancement of life. She embodies the comic force in action, guaranteeing man's unlimited possibilities for maturity and self-realization. To Lady Windermere's sentimental ideal of a "pure" mother, she opposes a critical awareness sharpened by the qualification of irony she gives to her daughter's illusions. Lady Windermere, however, still clings to her illusions despite the predicament she has undergone, despite her mother's belief: "ideals are dangerous things. Realities are better. They wound, but they are better."

One perceives how Mrs. Erlynne "manipulates" most of the action, from the moment Lord Windermere invites her to her daughter's birthday party to the moment she clears up the complication for the sake of the incredibly naive Lord Augustus, whose rattling indictment of fashionable society—"Demmed clubs . . . demmed everything!"—climaxes Mrs. Erlynne's striving to enter society. The play ends like a fairy tale: Mrs. Erlynne and Lord Augustus depart from England, the Windermeres escape to the idyllic rose garden at Selby where "the roses are white and red" —not of mixed, equivocal hues.

Does Lady Windermere change at all? We meet her first as a stiff, narrow-minded Puritan who can tell exactly what is wrong and what is right. She tolerates no compromise between good and evil. Her forte is the mouthing of grandiose abstractions: life is "a sacrament. Its ideal is Love. Its purification is sacrifice." If she is "good," she is unnaturally "hard": "If a woman really repents, she never wishes to return to the society that has made or seen her ruin." She reviles her mother by calling her "vile." Happily Wilde always undercuts her excessive, forced casuistry with his deflating playfulness:

LADY WINDERMERE: Because the husband is vile—should the wife be vile also?

LORD DARLINGTON: Vileness is a terrible word, Lady Windermere.
LADY WINDERMERE: It is a terrible thing, Lord Darlington.
LORD DARLINGTON: Do you know I am afraid that good people do a great
    deal of harm in this world. Certainly the greatest harm they do is
    that they make badness of such extraordinary importance. It is
    absurd to divide people into good and bad. People are either charm-
    ing or tedious. I take the side of the charming, and you, Lady
    Windermere, can't help belonging to them.

Ethical attitudes clash with "aesthetic" attitudes. Lady Windermere prides
herself in declaring that "I will have no one in my house about whom
there is any scandal," when almost all of her guests are either foppish or
despicable shams.

Characteristically Lady Windermere is associated with roses and
ideals. She boasts of her belief that "Windermere and I married for love."
Wilde parodies her in the figure of Agatha, with her "mechanical" innocence and "pure tastes." But life, as Lord Darlington reminds her, is "too
complex a thing to be settled by these hard and fast rules"; moreover, "life
is far too important a thing ever to talk seriously about it." By "seriously"
is meant "dogmatically." Experience then—"the name everyone gives to
their mistakes"—teaches by example; experience designates "instinct about
life." Lord Darlington asserts further: "Love changes" men. Lady Windermere partly changes her attitude in the last act, after her escape from what
would have been a compromising situation. She reflects thus: "How
securely one thinks one lives—out of reach of temptation, sin, folly. And
then suddenly—oh! life is terrible. It rules us, we do not rule it." Later on
her absolutism relaxes. Meanwhile, Lord Windermere, in his ignorance,
proceeds to condemn outright Mrs. Erlynne after the incident in the third
act. He shifts his position from extreme tolerance to legalistic sternness.
So his wife reproaches him with this bit of oratory:

> Arthur, Arthur, don't talk so bitterly about any woman. I don't think
> now that people can be divided into the good and the bad, as though
> they were two separate races or creations. What are called good women
> may have terrible things in them, mad moods of recklessness, assertion,
> jealousy, sin. Bad women, as they are termed, may have in them sorrow,
> repentance, pity, sacrifice. And I don't think Mrs. Erlynne a bad woman—I
> know she's not.

Her knowledge has the confirmation of experience. Although she still
sticks to her "ideals," she tones them down with a liberal generosity of
temper: "There is the same world for all of us, and good and evil, sin and
innocence, go through it hand in hand. To shut one's eyes to half of life
that one may live securely is as though one blinded oneself that one might
walk with more safety in a land of pit and precipice."

Wilde modifies the "long-lost-child" pattern by not following it to its customary end: the expected dénouement of recognition between child and parent. What results is that Lady Windermere, even after the ordeal, remains essentially the same as she was before: an exponent of illusions. Although she has learned to question her judgments, she has not learned to question her moral standards—the traditional categories of good and evil. She has not earned "the right to the truth," her conscience goes on to feed on "white and red" roses. For in the idyllic world of the self-complacent rich, things are clear and simple: only by testing and recasting their categories can men prove equal to the complexity of their experience.

Mrs. Erlynne, on the other hand, has preferred realities to ideals from the start. Lord Windermere's description that she is "a bad woman preying upon life" points to her "ferocity," which penetrates into social appearances and beyond them, into the realm of inward verities. Her spiritual encounters free her from the factitious and arbitrary rules of social existence. Lord Windermere suggests her inner suffering when he says: "Misfortunes one can endure—they come from outside, they are accidents. But to suffer for one's own faults—ah!—there is the sting of life." After realizing a mother's devotion to her child, she has more or less lived in a single moment what she had until then failed to experience; one existential moment redeems her. She has lost her honor "by a moment's folly": she recovers it by a moment's selflessness. Losing herself, she gains identity. At the moment of deciding to "save" Lady Windermere, she feels "a passion awakening within." In contrast, Lady Windermere is the pale "coward" who, though now "of age," cannot choose what she really wants for herself. Lord Darlington challenges her: "It is wrong for a wife to remain with a man who so dishonours her. You said once you would make no compromise with things. Make none now. Be brave! Be yourself!" Circumstances force her to decide; self-righteous indignation prods her to seek refuge in Lord Darlington's "friendship." Thus she forgets her mother's "past," compelled by the force of revulsion. Her birthday fan, which signifies her presumed "maturity," instead of being a weapon to strike her mother, becomes an instrument of escape. And so ultimately, her mother, her true origin, symbolized by the fan, saves her.

The recurrence of words like "save," "fall," "sin," "repent," "self-sacrifice," "know," and "understand," builds up the crucial scenes for spiritual commitment and renewal. It amplifies the comic idea of self-knowledge through one's courage, initiative, and charity. Lady Windermere flees from her husband because he has, she says, never "understood" her. On the other hand, Mrs. Erlynne is a woman who "thoroughly understands" people. Early in the play Lady Windermere evinces her crippling drawback when she refuses to know "details about" Mrs. Erlynne's life; she is responsible for her own dilemma. Lord Windermere speaks of Mrs. Erlynne's effort to "know" her daughter; on his part, he claims to "know" her thoroughly. In Act IV he believes her immorality to have been "found out." What the Windermeres lack is self-knowledge gained from self-detachment—an ideal which Dumby, by a form of understated boasting, exemplifies: "I am the only person in the world I should like to know thoroughly."

The dandy, whose vocation is the dissection of motives, upholds self-knowledge as a virtue in action. Lord Darlington, for example, confesses his "little vanities" frankly. He can either display "verbal wit" or fabricate "extravagant silly things." He regards "marriage as a game." Although he exhibits "affectations of weakness," the "weakness" is only a matter of affectation. Lord Augustus' statement that "none of us men do look what we really are" is a serious confession and a public indictment. Lord Darlington knows that sham and sincerity are relative: "If you pretend to be good, the world takes you very seriously. If you pretend to be bad, it doesn't. Such is the astounding stupidity of optimism." Bad or good, it's all a pretense. Lord Darlington may be an unscrupulous cad but his posture is more flexible and stimulating than that of the moralizing Windermeres. The play in effect proves the dandy's asphorism that "a man who moralizes is usually a hypocrite, and a woman who moralizes is invariably plain." Misunderstandings cause divisions and "chasms"; Mrs. Erlynne warns her daughter of the "abyss" on whose brink, "the brink of a hideous precipice," she now stands; below is the "life of degradation." In contrast, the dandy accepts the state of things; but his realism comprehends the ideal:

> DUMBY: I don't think we are bad. I think we are all good except Tuppy.
> LORD DARLINGTON: No, we are all in the gutter, but some of us are looking at the stars.

That last epigram, a memorable quip, stands out from the glib inanities of the drawing room talk.

Wilde's play presents a problem and, by the manipulation of events, solves it in a provisional fashion. The substance of the plot is composed largely of the conflict between men and women; the relationships of the sexes are constantly changing under pressure of criticism and argument. The Duchess of Berwick tells us that "all men are monsters." Lord Darlington defines the relation in terms of attraction and repulsion:

"Between men and women there is no friendship possible. There is passion, enmity, worship, love, but no friendship." But these conflicts life resolves: Lord Windermere accepts the role of accidents. Accidents bring us misfortunes; chance may reconcile, as suggested by the coincidence of Lady Windermere's and Mrs. Erlynne's Christian names: "What a wonderful chance our names being the same"—remarks Lady Windermere near the end.

Eventually Mrs. Erlynne "finds" herself by the felicitous interaction of circumstances. Because she desires to be accepted by society again, she manages to be "invited" to her daughter's party. The audience knows the situation; we know it too, and thereby a kind of reconciliation between the outcast and her past is effected. Mrs. Erlynne's effort is a quest for identity in a social setting; she has never really excluded herself from society because she has always acted in the light of the social condemnation of her past. Indeed, she testifies to the fact that nobody can be completely alone in the world. As Lady Windermere puts it to her husband: "You fancy because I have no father or mother that I am alone in the world and that you can treat me as you choose. I have friends, many friends." One of her friends is Lord Darlington, who proves "annoying" in positive and negative ways.

The drama principally centers on the relationship between Mrs. Erlynne and Lady Windermere, between mother and daughter. Driven inwardly to her ego, the daughter becomes "cold and loveless"; whereas driven to her inmost passionate self Mrs. Erlynne is able to perform an act of self-sacrifice "spontaneously, recklessly, nobly"—as her daughter describes it. Notice how the irony develops: Lord Windermere implores his wife to "save" Mrs. Erlynne; later, it turns out that Mrs. Erlynne has "saved" her daughter's honor, laboring under the fear that "the mask" of anonymity may be "stripped from one's face" by pathos and sentiment. The mother has no distinct "relations"; when Lady Windermere blurts out, "What have I to do with you?" she humbly responds: "Nothing." She adds later: "Our lives lie too far apart." She is known only as a woman with a past, but she finds that nothing has altered in society; "there are just as many fools in society as there used to be." Her act of love toward her daughter will always be kept a secret from the public. It was for the sake of preventing the repetition of her tragic life that she ignored her own interest when she rushed to Lord Darlington's room; but contrary to her belief that she is "lost," she has "found" herself—her mother-self. Finally explaining everything, as Lord Augustus testifies, Mrs. Erlynne "dances through life" with the poise that experience has given her.

"A WOMAN OF NO IMPORTANCE"

Wilde's second play, *A Woman of No Importance*, was written around September 1892 and produced at the Haymarket Theatre on April 19, 1893. The contemporary critic William Archer, on this occasion, pronounced Wilde's works "on the very highest plane of modern English drama." But this particular work has generally been ignored as trivial, although the texture of the dialogue and the thematic complications somehow rescue the plot from banality.

The titular heroine Mrs. Arbuthnot, like Mrs. Erlynne, harbors a "tainted" past. She represents the "fallen woman," a literary type of the century which reflects in part the insidious effects of a double standard of morality, the ruthless indifference to feminine welfare, and the seduction of lower-class girls by "gentlemen" of the upper class. But Mrs. Arbuthnot exists as a personality in her own right. She resolutely safeguards her past disgrace from oblivion; after twenty years, she still cannot forgive the villain Lord Illingworth, who now wants to take their son Gerald away from her. In the last act, Mrs. Arbuthnot inflates her glorious hardships for the sake of her son, in her speech beginning with "Men don't understand what mothers are." Accepting "heavy punishments and great disgrace," she discovers that Gerald, the fruit of her sin, is her only wealth. She says that though her seducer dishonored her, yet he "left me richer, so that in the mire of my life I have found the pearl of price." Because of this she has never really repented; her son was worth more than innocence. She says:

> I would rather be your mother—oh! much rather—than have been always pure. . . . It is my dishonour that has made you so dear to me. It is my disgrace that has bound you so closely to me. It is the price I paid for you—the price of soul and body—that makes me love you as I do.

What Mrs. Arbuthnot expects from her acquiescence to fate and the painful humiliations she has suffered is that her son will "repay" her sooner or later. Mrs. Arbuthnot, like most women victimized by an illicit passion, seems to have become a degraded "promissory note," a property of the young Lord Illingworth. "Promissory note" is the phrase given by the flirtatious Mrs. Allonby to her husband. For Lady Caroline, the Ideal Man "has to do nothing but pay bills and compliments"—a juxtaposition found also in *Lady Windermere's Fan*. We are once more involved in the measurement of human relationships not according to the "give-and-take" of affection but according to a calculus of advantage and disadvantage, investment and dividend. We are involved with the "mercantile" motive that initially animates Mrs. Erlynne's virtues in the preceding play, and that of Mrs. Cheveley in *An Ideal Husband*. In contrast with her counterparts, Mrs. Arbuthnot belongs to "the good, sweet, simple people"—to quote Lady Hunstanton—who live within the "sensible system" and "artificial social barriers" of English society.

Associated with this motif of "paying" and "repaying" is the idea of "saving" and "losing." Mrs. Arbuthnot, for instance, claims the "saving" of Lord Illingworth from the murderous rage of her son Gerald, who vowed to kill him after he dared to kiss Hester on a bet with Mrs. Allonby. Later she tells Lord Illingworth: "We are safe from you, and we are going away." We find other connotations of "save," aside from "protecting," in this exchange in the last act:

> GERALD: . . . I would die to save you. But you don't tell me what to do now!
> HESTER: Have I not thanked you for saving me?

She has been saved from a dandy's rudeness but not from her shallow attitude to life, which has not anticipated such a violent act coming from a person with an elegant, respectable façade. Gerald has saved Hester from Lord Illingworth's "joke," though the dandy's attempt on her virtue, like the Devil's on Eve's, is rather expected. Lady Caroline, one recalls, mentions America as "the Paradise of women," to which Lord Illingworth replies: "It is, Lady Caroline. That is why, like Eve, they are so extremely anxious to get out of it." From what is Mrs. Arbuthnot safe? Certainly not from the good intentions of Lord Illingworth, who only wants to insure his son's stable future. To bring about his father's atonement, Gerald conceives of a "reparation": Lord Illingworth should marry his mother. But Mrs. Arbuthnot's mind is fixed: "What should I have done in honest households? My past was ever with me. . . ." Gerald, chivalric and prudent, seeks to vindicate his mother's honor and to realize justice within social norms; he urges his mother thus: "You must marry him. It is your duty."

Despite much preaching and sentimentalizing on her part Mrs. Arbuthnot, first uncertain in her decision, finally resolves to be firm in her refusal to forgive the erring dandy. This comes after the wealthy Hester proclaims her support of Mrs. Arbuthnot's stand. Both women then deliver grandiloquent speeches that seem out of proportion to the problem they face. Although twenty years have elapsed since her fatal passion; although Gerald now is already able to support himself, and Lord Illingworth prepared to "rehabilitate" her, Mrs. Arbuthnot still wants the past to prevail. She and Hester obfuscate the situation by their sentimental rhetoric:

> HESTER (running forward and embracing Mrs. Arbuthnot): . . . Leave him and come with me. There are other countries than England. . . .

> Oh! other countries over the sea, better, wiser, and less unjust lands. The world is very wide and very big.
>
> MRS. ARBUTHNOT: No, not for me. For me the world is shrivelled to a palm's breadth, and where I walk there are thorns.

But their proposals are not solutions; in fact, they evade the problem. They are simply displays of mawkishness incited by floating abstractions. Wilde doesn't even justify Hester's radical change from dogmatic Puritan to charitable evangelist—unless Lord Illingworth's rudeness has quickly led her to identify herself with his former victim Mrs. Arbuthnot.

Set these exaggerations beside the dandy's metallic epigrams, and we grasp the central opposing forces in the play: feeling *versus* logic. Mrs. Allonby, in Act II, says that "there is something positively brutal about the good temper of most modern men"; Lady Stutfield replies: "Yes; men's good temper shows they are not so sensitive as we are, not so finely strung. It makes a great barrier often between husband and wife, does it not?" This opposition between reason and feeling, between the detached "dandy" and the sensitive woman, is conveyed to us in a straightforward manner:

> LADY CAROLINE: . . . It is much to be regretted that in our rank of life the wife should be so persistently frivolous, under the impression apparently that it is the proper thing to be. It is to that I attribute the unhappiness of so many marriages we all know of in society.
>
> MRS. ALLONBY: Do you know, Lady Caroline, I don't think the frivolity of the wife has ever anything to do with it. More marriages are ruined nowadays by the common sense of the husband than by anything else. How can a woman be expected to be happy with a man who insists on treating her as if she were a perfectly rational being?

Lord Illingworth epitomizes the virtue of "common sense" in his offer of marriage with Mrs. Arbuthnot for the sake of their son's future. But she persists in her self-indulgent "humor"; she proves his opinion that "women are a fascinatingly wilful sex." In Act III, Lord Illingworth tells Gerald: ". . . to the philosopher, women represent the triumph of mind over morals. . . . Nothing refines but the intellect." When in Act II, he and Mrs. Arbuthnot first meet, he displays his calm in contrast to her nervousness:

> My dear Rachel, intellectual generalizations are always interesting, but generalities in morals mean absolutely nothing. As for saying I left our child to starve, that, of course, is untrue and silly. My mother offered you six hundred a year. But you wouldn't take anything. You simply disappeared, and carried the child away with you.

He gives the edge to his argument when he tries to dissociate the mother's past from the son's future, scolding Mrs. Arbuthnot thus:

> What a typical woman you are! You talk sentimentally, and you are
> thoroughly selfish the whole time. But don't let us have a scene. Rachel,
> I want you to look at this matter from the common-sense point of view,
> from the point of view of what is best for our son, leaving you and me
> out of the question.

Which is just precisely what Mrs. Arbuthnot cannot do. She cannot
dispense with her possessive attitude toward her son ("my son"). She
therefore refuses to compromise, rejoicing in her "tragic" burden, in her
"sin." *She* does not think, she responds by impulse and sheer feminine
intuition.

Earlier Lord Illingworth has expressed the idea that "all thought is
immoral. It's the very essence of destruction. If you think of anything, you
kill it. Nothing survives being thought of." "We are all heart, all heart,"
Lady Hunstanton suggests, believing that all mothers are weak. Women—
Mrs. Arbuthnot observes—are hard on each other, perhaps because they
are all "heart" and lack detachment. Take, for example, Hester's categorical judgments: "Let all women who have sinned be punished. . . ." Lord
Illingworth, in his ambiguous witticisms, recognizes the dualism of rational and instinctive qualities: "Nothing is serious except passion. The
intellect is not a serious thing, and never has been. It is an instrument on
which one plays, that is all." On the intellect as an instrument Lord
Illingworth plays craftily, to the discomfiture of Lady Hunstanton and her
kind. The Lady herself remarks: "Personally I have very little to reproach
myself with, on the score of thinking. I don't believe in women thinking
too much."

Hester Worsley embodies the rigid position that women tend to
take with respect to moral questions. She seems to conform to that prosaic
image of the American woman Wilde describes in a review: "There is
something fascinating in their funny exaggerated gestures and their petulant way of tossing the head. Their eyes have no magic nor mystery in
them but they challenge us for combat; and when we engage we are always
worsted." Hester fits into the humorless category of women for whom
"there is neither romance nor humility in her love." She is not only
"painfully natural," as Lady Stutfield refers to her embarrassing candor;
but she is also pretentious in her righteousness. She declaims sancti-
moniously amid the flippant chatter of dowagers. Lady Caroline's remark
at the end of her speech, in its timely juxtaposition, deflates at once
Hester's solemn rant:

> HESTER: It is right that they should be punished but don't let them be the
>   only ones to suffer. If a man and woman have sinned, let them both
>   go forth into the desert to love or loathe each other. Let them both

be branded. Set a mark, if you wish, on each, but don't punish the one and let the other go free. Don't have one law for men and another for women. You are unjust to women in England. And till you count what is a shame in a woman to be an infamy in a man, you will always be unjust, and Right, that pillar of fire, and Wrong, that pillar of cloud, will be made dim to your eyes, or be not seen at all, or if seen, not regarded.

LADY CAROLINE: Might I, dear Miss Worsley, as you are standing up, ask you for my cotton that is just behind you? Thank you.

Wilde's fertile inventiveness provides a mode of fulfilling his impulse for exhibitionism, for the ostentatious show of his virtuosity. A variety of texture and tone in speech results. Hester's flamboyance and pompous solemnity contrasts with the pithy epigrams of Lord Illingworth (e.g., "Nothing succeeds like excess"). The dry, elegant aphorisms of Wilde's dandies seem to infect the conversation of the other characters in the comedies. In the case of Lord Illingworth, his engaging wit redeems his callousness, his coarseness and vulgarity. On the other hand, there is something distasteful in Hester's stern pronouncements, which make her into an unlikely sage of eighteen. Mrs. Arbuthnot, like Hester, has a flair for flatulent oratory; she tends to convert pathos into a sticky fudge of verbiage. In between the thunderous curtains we listen to the pedestrian drivel of "the mindless boors" and "sycophantic cronies." A typical verbal trick of substitution occurs in the mannerisms of some of the "flat" characters, in Dr. Daubeny's repetitions, or in Lady Hunstanton's forgetfulness: "I was in hopes he would have married Lady Kelso. But I believe he said her family was too large. Or was it her feet?" saying that Lady Belton had eloped with Lord Fethersdale, she adds, "Poor Lord Belton died three days afterwards of joy, or gout. I forget which. . . ."

After Hester has observed and heard Mrs. Arbuthnot, she relaxes her obstinate casuistry a bit, confessing to her future mother-in-law: "When you came into the drawing-room this evening, somehow you brought with you a sense of what is good and pure in life. I had been foolish. There are things that are right to say, but that may be said at the wrong time and to the wrong people." But though she may adjust herself to the situation, her corresponding attitudes remain fixed: "It is right that the sins of the parents should be visited on the children." Later she amends this "just" law. After Lord Illingworth's attempt to kiss her, and in her sympathy with the anguished Mrs. Arbuthnot, Hester now believes that "God's law is only Love."

Such a change in thinking springs from Hester's emotional susceptibility: she is either totally angry or totally sympathetic. Her moods and affections easily influence her judgments. Mrs. Arbuthnot, unlike Hester, alters her decisions in consonance with her attachment to her past. Reminded by her son, in Act II, that she is also in part guilty of her youthful "indiscretion," she yields to Gerald's wish; in Act III, however, she reverses her decision. While Gerald seeks to reconcile his parents in marriage, his mother, in righteous indignation, elects a double standard and affirms the inequality of fate between men and women: "It is the usual history of a man and a woman, as it usually happens, as it always happens. And the ending is the ordinary ending. The woman suffers. The man goes free." This view prevents her from allowing for the imperfections of men and the absurdities of experience. Her judgments run on one track, permitting no possibility of growth or improvement in the process of life. She denies the possibility of an inward change in the character of Lord Illingworth: "It is not what Lord Illingworth believes, or what he does not believe, that makes him bad. It is what he is." The recollection of the past seems to reduce her sensibility into a stasis of empty despair, which she rationalizes by her lachrymose portrayals of her suffering as a martyr of womankind. She is almost redundant in her reactions, which one can easily predict. In short, she can easily be "typed":

> GERALD: Is it fair to go back twenty years in any man's career? And what
>   have you or I to do with Lord Illingworth's early life? What business
>   is it of ours?
> MRS. ARBUTHNOT: What this man has been, he is now, and will be always.

Evidently she is trying to liken him to herself in her stubborn clinging to her guilty past. Consequently she thinks of her "sin" as being visited on her innocent child. Nothing has changed for her in twenty years; one can even say that she has indulged in her role as victim. Whereas to Lord Illingworth "what is over is over," to Mrs. Arbuthnot the past lives on as a perpetual curse hovering in the air wherever she goes:

> MRS. ARBUTHNOT: . . . You don't realise what my past has been in
>   suffering and in shame.
> LORD ILLINGWORTH: My dear Rachel, I must candidly say that I think
>   Gerald's future considerably more important than your past.
> MRS. ARBUTHNOT: Gerald cannot separate his future from my past.

Now Lord Illingworth, who corresponds to the conception of the Ideal Man because he is—as Lady Caroline says—"extremely realistic," is a man of compromise. His intelligence comprehends opposing views. It can turn platitudes topsy-turvy and still preserve its validity in application to life. His talent is directed toward refining the "art of living." To him modern life signifies being "fit for the best society. . . . Society is a necessary thing. No man has any real success in this world unless he has got women to back him, and women rule society. Accepting the passage of time and its psychological impact, Lord Illingworth perceives with greater intensity the value of youth, youth having "a kingdom waiting for it." He declares, "saints have a past, sinners have a future." He calls his looking glass "unkind" because "it merely shows my wrinkles." But his flexibility and generosity of temper could not influence the closed mind of Mrs. Arbuthnot. In the end he yields to a retrospective mood; all morality and prudence vanish, and he sees in Mrs. Arbuthnot only "the prettiest of playthings, the most fascinating of small romances. . . ."

In general, comic characters are those whose attitudes and outlook in life are out of proportion to, and so falsify, the actualities of experience. They appear ridiculous in their exaggeration of certain ideas and sentiments without reference to the flux of circumstances. They adhere blindly to limited positions, heedless of time and the potencies for growth and inward change in man. Wilde thus criticizes Mrs. Arbuthnot's bondage to her past. Her past is indirectly diminished in importance by the famous forgetfulness of Lady Hunstanton, and by the infantile regression of Mrs. Daubeny, who recalls chiefly "the events of her childhood" after her last attack of illness. Wilde projects the idea of life's development in Gerald's grasping of "my one chance in life," his "wonderful piece of good luck." He entertains the prospect of being Lord Illingworth's secretary. Lord Illingworth is a man who commands great power and resources: "there is nothing he couldn't get if he chose to ask for it." To his pleas that Gerald and he be brought together, Mrs. Arbuthnot replies: "There can be nothing in common between you and my son." But Gerald wants to be like his father, expressing the same temperament, cherishing similar ambitions. He likes Lord Illingworth's "cleverness, prosperity, and self-confidence." He asserts his freedom to choose and make "a position" for himself in the world.

In life as well as in comedy, time has a way of playing tricks that affect the destiny of individuals. Lord Illingworth says at one point that he has "found" his son. Words like "know," "mean," and the like, connote concealment and discovery. For example, Lord Illingworth says to Gerald, "I want you to know how to live." Gerald says to his father: "I want you so much to know my mother." Mrs. Allonby says of the "Ideal Man": "He should always say much more than he means, and always mean much more than he says. . . ." Mrs. Arbuthnot maintains throughout that her meeting with Lord Illingworth "was a mere accident, a horrible accident." She cannot make the sacrifice of allowing her son to choose for himself, to *know* himself. In Act II Mrs. Arbuthnot comes in "unannounced" by way of the terrace; she is described as living too much "out of the world." She is the outsider who penetrates "artificial social barriers." Lord Illingworth confesses to having concealed the truth from the world; from society's standpoint she is a "woman of no importance." Ultimately she refuses to abide by the dynamic rhythm of life in which accidents—such as Hester's casting her fortune with them—play a great role. To assume with her that "all love is terrible" and is a "tragedy" would be to condemn automatically Gerald's and Hester's alliance. In the end she succumbs to a self-engendered paralysis, dominating her son's will, and purging herself of warmth and kindness: "My heart is cold: something has broken it."

From another viewpoint Mrs. Arbuthnot appears to have grasped the opportunity presented by Hester's wealth. Paradoxically she resolves Gerald's problem by comforming to the social standard of wealth and material security. Her heart belongs to the "good, sweet, simple people" on whom the dandy's destructive energy feeds in its affirmation of life's capacity for change and development. Ultimately Lord Illingworth's vision reconciles life's discords in its recognition of incongruity: "the world has always laughed at its own tragedies, that being the only way in which it has been able to bear them. And that, consequently, whatever the world has treated seriously belongs to the comedy side of things."

"AN IDEAL HUSBAND"

Wilde's least successful play on the stage and his third comedy, *An Ideal Husband,* was written between October 1893 and March 1894. It was produced at the Haymarket Theatre on January 3, 1895. When Wilde in 1899 corrected the proofs of the play for publication, he said that it "reads rather well, and some of its passages seem prophetic of tragedy to come." But Sir Robert Chiltern's predicament, though it bears a tenuous resemblance to Wilde's, has distinctive melodramatic overtones.

The play concerns itself primarily with Sir Robert Chiltern's past misdeed on which his fortune and eminent reputation now stand. The past, in the form of Mrs. Cheveley's immoral ends, revives in order to haunt and threaten him. Just as, in the three other plays, the past proves a force that motivates the thematic action, so here time seems to be the concept that governs the complication and resolution of the plot. The play deals with the problem of how well man, confronted with the alterable modes of his life, can adjust or adapt himself to the needs of changing situations. Where an absolute standard is obeyed despite the criticism of it by experience and actuality, there result irony, distortions, and absurdities that arouse ridicule and laughter.

Notice first how the scenes of the play shift from the "social" crowded atmosphere of the Octagon Room at Chiltern's house (Act I) to a "private" room (Act II), then to the secluded library of Lord Goring where the two letters—the fatal letter of Sir Robert Chiltern and Lady Chiltern's letter to Lord Goring—play decisive roles. The scene finally returns to the setting of Act II, where social and private interests intersect; where all the rough, disturbing edges of the misunderstanding between husband and wife are smoothed off by obvious devices—by means of the diamond brooch that Lord Goring uses to restrain Mrs. Cheveley, and by Mrs. Cheveley's stupidity in not explaining to Chiltern the nature of the letter his wife wrote to Lord Goring. Eventually the play closes with a sense of new life for the Chilterns, while Lord Goring and Mabel Chiltern entertain the prospect of a happy marriage. The image of a stable society prevails in the end, as the conventions of marriage, family life, and public office are severally affirmed.

When Act I opens, Mrs. Marchmont and Lady Basildon, "types of exquisite fragility," display their "affectations of manner" which, however, do not make their remarks pointless:

> MRS. MARCHMONT: Horribly tedious parties they give, don't they?
> LADY BASILDON: Horribly tedious! Never know why I go. Never know why I go anywhere.

Mabel Chiltern states in ironic terms the combination of polished form and hollow insides that society presents: "Oh, I love London society! I think it has immensely improved. It is entirely composed now of beautiful idiots and brilliant lunatics. Just what society should be." Her indictment gains pungent venom in Lord Caversham's opinion that London society "has gone to the dogs, a lot of damned nobodies talking about nothing."

Dress or fashion furnishes an index to social attitudes and values. Lord Goring pronounces: "fashion is what one wears oneself. What is unfashionable is what other people wear." When he offers to give Mrs. Cheveley "some good advice," she replies: "Oh! pray don't. One should never give a woman anything that she can't wear in the evening." The interest in appearance occupies the foreground in this exchange:

> MRS. CHEVELEY (languidly): I have never read a Blue Book. I prefer books . . . in yellow covers.
> LADY MARKBY (genially unconscious): Yellow is a gayer colour, is it not? I used to wear yellow a good deal in my early days, and would do so now if Sir John was not so painfully personal in his observations, and a man on the question of dress is always ridiculous, is he not?

Politics is a kind of "fashion," too, in its concern with public appearance. Lady Basildon claims to talk politics ceaselessly. Sir Robert Chiltern regards a political life as "a noble career," though our knowledge of his past belies his statement. But in the political or practical life, the criterion of success reduces moral standards to the basic level of pragmatic efficacy. As Lord Goring puts it, "in practical life there is something about success, actual success, that is a little unscrupulous, something about ambition that is unscrupulous always."

In Act IV, Lady Chiltern believes that Sir Robert's ambition has led him astray in his early days. She says that "power is nothing in itself. It is power to do good that is fine." Her husband admits to Lord Goring that he "bought success at a great price." And yet he is highly esteemed for being a respectable, selfless "public servant," a model of virtue, which is but a "front" or mask that he wears in conformity to social norms. After all, as Lord Goring remarks, almost all private fortune in society has come from dubious "speculation." On knowing her husband's guilt, Lady Chiltern hysterically complains not of his pretense but of his inability to "lie" to her for the sake of "virtues" he has been socially known for. Lady Chiltern cries out,

> Don't touch me. I feel as if you had soiled me forever. Oh! what a mask you have been wearing all these years! A horrible, painted mask! You sold yourself for money. Oh! a common thief were better. You put yourself up for sale to the highest bidder! You were bought in the market. You lied to the whole world. And yet you will not lie to me!

This exposure means a stripping of costume, an "undressing," to disclose the authentic self. One recalls Lady Markby's experience, which prefigures Sir Robert's plight, when she describes the result of immersion in the crowd:

> The fact is, we all scramble and jostle so much nowadays that I wonder we have anything at all left on us at the end of an evening. I know myself that, when I am coming back from the Drawing Room, I always feel as if I hadn't a shred on me, except a small shred of decent reputation just enough to prevent the lower classes making painful observations through the windows of the carriage.

Behind Sir Robert's open "goodness" lies a secret "truth," the as yet unacknowledged truth of human frailty. He has committed an immoral act in order to insure his social success.

Act I gives us the needed background information about the moral issue. Mrs. Cheveley remarks: "Nowadays, with our modern mania for morality, everyone has to pose as a paragon of purity, incorruptibility, and all the other seven deadly virtues." She threatens Sir Robert:

> Yours is a very nasty scandal. You couldn't survive it. If it were known that as a young man, secretary to a great and important minister, you sold a Cabinet secret for a large sum of money, and that was the origin of your wealth and career, you would be hounded out of public life, you would disappear completely. . . . You have a splendid position but it is your splendid position that makes you so vulnerable.

She elaborates on the punishment that the fallen victim is bound to receive from society:

> Suppose that when I leave this house I drive down to some newspaper office, and give them this scandal and the proofs of it! I think of their loathsome joy, of the delight they would have in dragging you down, of the mud and mire they would plunge you in. Think of the hypocrite with his greasy smile penning his leading article, and arranging the foulness of the public placard.

Ironically Lady Chiltern thinks that her husband has no "secrets" from her.

Confronted with his "shameful" secret, Sir Robert Chiltern reflects on how most men have "worse secrets in their own lives." Lord Goring himself, in planning to thwart Mrs. Cheveley's designs, believes that "everyone has some weak point. There is some flaw in each one of us." Aware of human limitations, he allows for imperfections in men. Observation, if not experience, has taught him that the "ideal husband" is a myth. He says to Lady Chiltern in Act II:

> I have sometimes thought that . . . perhaps you are a little hard in some of your views on life. I think that . . . often you don't make sufficient allowances.In every nature there are elements of weakness, or worse than weakness.

Just as Sir Robert has a "past," so does his enemy Mrs. Cheveley. She ceases to be a mystery when Lady Chiltern recalls her as a schoolmate: "She was untruthful, dishonest, an evil influence on everyone whose trust or friendship she could win. . . . She stole things, she was a thief. She was sent away for being a thief." Lord Goring discovers later that she has stolen the diamond brooch he has given to a friend. Thus Mrs. Cheveley is not without her secret crime, of which Lord Goring accuses her later. Her image as an intriguing woman who "makes great demands on one's curiosity" is soon modified by the knowledge we get of her past life, her origin; she, who claims to possess integrity, turns out to be an embodiment of corruption.

It seems that the past, what is dead and forgotten, is always valuable for the perspective of the comic vision. The past qualifies man's pride; it gives an objective picture of any man's life. Whereas the past judges man in his finitude, the future gives him the freedom of choosing his possible, ideal selves. Mrs. Cheveley proves the most vulnerable character because, as she declares, her "memory is under admirable control." The one real tragedy in a woman's life, she says, is the fact that "her past is always her lover, and her future invariably her husband." Sir Robert, of course, is the "man" with a future, as Mabel Chiltern says; but his future rests on his past. When Mrs. Cheveley enters the scene, he starts reflecting on life:

> It is fair that the folly, the sin of one's youth, if men choose to call it a sin, should wreck a life like mine, should place me in the pillory, should shatter all that I have worked for, all that I have built up? Is it fair, Arthur?

Lord Goring replies: "Life is never fair, Robert. And perhaps it is a good thing for most of us that it is not."

What is the danger that life confronts us with? It is the danger of having an open mind, an equipoise within, a balance which comes from a just calculation of the factors that affect one's life. When Lord Goring suggests that Sir Robert alter his wife's fixed views on life, Sir Robert replies: "All such experiments are terribly dangerous." Lord Goring, however, counters: "Everything is dangerous, my dear fellow. If it wasn't so, life wouldn't be worth living." He entertains, in short, the surprises and novelties that organic life is ever producing. In Act IV, life puts Lady Chiltern's reputation in danger. We see how Sir Robert becomes desperate, then panicked: "I clutch at every chance. I feel like a man on a ship that is sinking." The disaster being still on the level of conjecture, his interjections are maudlin: "My life seems to have crumbled about me. I am a ship without a rudder in a night without a star." This radically qualifies the role of Sir Robert as a man with a "serious purpose in life," a "pattern husband." Lady Chiltern amplifies her husband's image:

> A man's life is of more value than a woman's. It has larger issues, wider scope, greater ambitions. Our lives revolve in curves of emotions. It is upon lines of intellect that a man's life progresses.

"Lines of intellect" versus "curves of emotion"—this opposition involves society's failure to establish harmonious relations between men and women. It involves a milieu in which the accepted codes of behavior do not promote the sensibility of men to function integrally. Wilde's portrayal of his "ideal husband" sets directly the contrast between feeling and conscious thought, between perceived behavior and the groping, reckless inner self:

> The note of his manner is that of perfect distinction, with a slight touch of pride. One feels that he is conscious of the success he has made in life. A nervous temperament, with a tired look. The firmly chiselled mouth and chin contrast strikingly with the romantic expression in the deep-set eyes. The variance is suggestive of an almost complete separation of passion and intellect, as though thought and emotion were each isolated in its own sphere through some violence of will-power.

Sir Robert Chiltern speaks in character when he insists on the idea of a compartmentalized life: ". . . public and private life are different things. They have different laws, and move on different lines."

Elsewhere men are called "horribly selfish" and "grossly material." Despite Sir Robert Chiltern's show of qualms and vacillation, Mrs. Cheveley is assured that he is "most susceptible to reason"—by which she means that he readily succumbs to fear of social disapproval. Women are gifted with "the moral sense." Lady Markby prefers anything other than "high intellectual pressure." To Lord Caversham, "common sense is the privilege" of men; in his view, marriage is a matter not of affection but of common sense. Mrs. Cheveley herself separates "business" from "silver twilights or rose-pink dawns." She considers being "natural" the most difficult pose of all. She holds that there is a wide gap between the rational method of science and the irrational layer of experience:

> MRS. CHEVELEY: Ah! the strength of women comes from the fact that psychology cannot explain us. Men can be analyzed, women . . . merely adored.
>
> SIR ROBERT CHILTERN: You think science cannot grapple with the problem of women?
>
> MRS. CHEVELEY: Science can never grapple with the irrational. That is why it has no future before it, in this world.
>
> SIR ROBERT CHILTERN: And women represent the irrational.
>
> MRS. CHEVELEY: Well-dressed women do.

The double aspects of life seem to be focused in Mrs. Cheveley's mysterious identity. Lord Goring describes her as "a genius in the daytime and a beauty at night." She plays with the attitudes of optimism and pessimism. What after all is the real self of a person? Lady Chiltern cannot believe her husband to be guilty of dreadful things which are "so unlike [his] real self." Her idealized image of him is that he has "brought into the political life of our time a nobler atmosphere, a finer attitude towards life, a freer air of purer aims and higher ideals." But reality is never as simple and pure as Lady Chiltern would like to imagine it. Society has become "dreadfully mixed" for Mrs. Cheveley; Lady Markby, likewise, observes that "families are so mixed nowadays. Indeed, as a rule, everybody turns out to be somebody else." Just as society is complex, so truth—as Sir Robert Chiltern believes—is a very complex thing.

To the unbending, puritanical Lady Chiltern, life however appears simple and fixed. She has always been noted for her stingy exclusiveness and conservatism. She has remained unaffected by changing circumstances:

> MRS. CHEVELEY: I see that after all these years you have not changed a bit, Gertrude.
> LADY CHILTERN: I never change.
> MRS. CHEVELEY (elevating her eyebrows): Then life has taught you nothing?
> LADY CHILTERN: It has taught me that a person who has once been guilty of a dishonest and dishonorable action may be guilty of it a second time and should be shunned.
> MRS. CHEVELEY: Would you apply that rule to everyone?
> LADY CHILTERN: Yes, to everyone, without exception.

We know of course that Sir Robert has changed. Mrs. Cheveley, though shrewder and more worldly-wise, has not reformed her ways. With firm logic Lady Chiltern holds to her conviction that human beings are what they are, past or present; that human nature is predestined, and is permanently fixed. She accuses Mrs. Cheveley of being dishonest on the basis of her past conduct:

> SIR ROBERT CHILTERN: Gertrude, what you tell me may be true, but it happened many years ago. It is best forgotten! Mrs. Cheveley may have changed since then. No one should be entirely judged by his past.
> LADY CHILTERN (sadly): One's past is what one is. It is the only way by which people should be judged.
> SIR ROBERT CHILTERN: That is a hard saying, Gertrude!
> LADY CHILTERN: It is a true saying, Robert. . . .

Like her counterparts in the other plays, Lady Windermere and Hester Worsley, Lady Chiltern does not believe that the sinner can make amends or work for his redemption. Addicted to histrionics, she often forgets the harsh prosaic facts of experience which are necessary to obtain an adequate understanding of human nature.

In contrast with her tolerant husband, Lady Chiltern acts without regard for the variable situations of life. Sir Robert Chiltern, it must be stressed, conceives himself changed since his early indiscretion on the ground that "circumstances alter things." But his wife decrees otherwise:

"Circumstances should never alter principles." Nonetheless, life's circumstances play a joke on her: when Sir Robert, in Act I, asks Mrs. Cheveley what brought her into his life in order to destroy his reputation and family honor, she answers: "Circumstances." Accident makes Robert negligent to the extent that he leaves the incriminating letter in Baron Arnheim's possession. And the accident of circumstance makes Mrs. Cheveley drop her diamond brooch, thus giving Lord Goring a weapon to prove her guilty of theft. On the whole, life offers chances to qualify, change, or confirm the truths and beliefs men hold. Sir Robert, for instance, speaks of the "wonderful chance" the Baron gave him to enrich himself unscrupulously. Later, he would bank on the "chance" that some scandal might be found involving his blackmailer Mrs. Cheveley. Desperately he exclaims: "Oh! I live on hopes now. I clutch at every chance."

We have noted previously the objective of success as a controlling force in Sir Robert's life. Early in his career he has been told that "luxury was nothing but background, a painted scene in a play"; what matters is power based on wealth. To be sure, he has never truly regretted his youthful crime. But the opportunity to acquire wealth unscrupulously he denies to others. Success, the chief social criterion of value, is parodied in the humorous puns on "triumph"; for example, Mabel Chiltern mentions a tableau in which she and Lady Chiltern are participants:

> You remember, we are having a tableaux, don't you? The triumph of something, I don't know what! I hope it will be the triumph of me. Only triumph I am really interested in at present.

Wilde describes the stage decoration in Act I: "Over the well of the staircase hangs a great chandelier with wax lights, which illumine a large eighteenth century French tapestry—representing the Triumph of Love, from a design by Boucher—that is stretched on the staircase wall." At the close of Act III, we see Mrs. Cheveley's face "illumined with evil triumph." What triumphs of course is the comic situation.

If the function of comedy is to reaffirm due proportion in life and restore "the golden mean," it is imperative that the "rules" for social existence be carefully defined. An attempt at this definition exists in Wilde's play. Sir Robert tries to expose Mrs. Cheveley's plan for a "swindle" instead of a "speculation": "let us call things by their proper names." Eventually she turns the table over him:

> SIR ROBERT CHILTERN: It is infamous, what you propose—infamous!
> MRS. CHEVELEY: Oh, no! This is the game of life as we all have to play it,
>   Sir Robert, sooner or later.

When he agrees on a bargain, with his support of her speculation in exchange for the incriminating letter, she says: "I intend to play quite fairly with you. One should always play fairly . . . when one has the winning cards."

Both the "game of life" and blackmail suggest commercial exchange, bargaining, profit and loss. Allusions and metaphors drawn from trade and finance are interwoven in the verbal fabric of the play. In Act I, Mrs. Cheveley appraises people according to their "price": "My dear Sir Robert, you are a man of the world, and you have your price, I suppose. Everybody has nowadays. The drawback is that most people are so dreadfully expensive." Later she exhorts him: "Years ago you did a clever, unscrupulous thing; it turned out a great success. You owe it to your fortune and position. And now you have got to pay for it. Sooner or later we all have to pay for what we do. You have to pay now." Offered a bribe, she refuses: "Even you are not rich enough, Sir Robert, to buy back your past. No man is." To Lady Chiltern, "money that comes from a tainted source is a degradation." Sir Robert confesses that while he did not sell himself for money, he "bought success at a great price." Lord Goring thinks that he "paid a great price for it." In his remorse, Sir Robert Chiltern vows that he has "paid conscience money many times" for his mistake. Mrs. Cheveley's transaction with Sir Robert, in Lord Goring's opinion, is a "loathsome commercial transaction of a loathsome commercial age." Mrs. Cheveley admits that much: "It is a commercial transaction. That is all. There is no good mixing up sentimentality in it. I offered to sell Robert Chiltern a certain thing. If he won't pay me my price, he will have to pay the world a greater price."

So in the middle of the play Sir Robert Chiltern is threatened with scandal and ruin because of what he did in the past. He declares that he has fought the century with its own weapon, wealth. He has shown the courage, cunning, and strength to yield to temptations: "To stake all one's life on a single moment, to risk everything on one throw, whether the stake be power or pleasure, I care not—there is no weakness in that. There is a horrible, terrible courage." Lord Goring's dandyism, his allowances for human vices and shortcomings, vindicate Sir Robert's resolution to defy Mrs. Cheveley. When Mrs. Cheveley boasts that she knows Sir Robert's "real character" by virtue of his letter, Lord Goring replies: "What you know about him is not his real character. It was an act of folly done in his youth, dishonourable, I admit, shameful, I admit, unworthy of him, I admit, and therefore . . . not his true character." Of the Chilterns' intended withdrawal from public life despite his promotion to a Cabinet post, Lord Goring remarks: "We men and women are not made to accept such sacrifices from each other. We are not worthy of them."

In the "flawless dandy" Lord Goring, we perceive the lineaments of "the ideal husband"—at least to Mabel Chiltern, in the future. He has a humaneness absent from his literary predecessors like Lord Henry Wotton, Lord Darlington, and Lord Illingworth. The dandy, in general, enacts the cult of the self not only in thought but also in the taste for dress and material elegance. He supports ceremony and social manners in principle. If he is anarchic, that is because he feels secure within the confines of society. Gestures and dress suggest the rhythm and harmony of a mind which depends on "the peculiar pleasure of astonishing and the proud satisfaction of never being astonished." Seriousness, or hypocrisy, is the "unbecoming" cardinal vice. As a clown armed with trivialities, the dandy exemplifies the value of external form as the emblem of what is within the self; he dissolves any disparity between the moral and the physical aspects of life. Lord Goring, in particular, abhors all romantic ideals, just as the dandies of the other comedies do. Pursuing a "gentleman's" routine, he exhibits "all the delicate fopperies of Fashion." Compared with Phipps the "ideal butler," the "mask with a manner," who represents "the dominance of form," Lord Goring has *élan vital*: "He plays with life, and is on perfectly good terms with the world. . . . One sees that he stands in immediate relation to modern life, makes it indeed, and so masters it." Mabel Chiltern, whose good sense springs from a feeling for just proportion in matters of daily life, does not desire Lord Goring to be an "ideal husband." For she feels that "he can be what he chooses"; her only wish is to be "a real wife to him." The significance of the adjective "real" inheres in a flexibility of attitude to life, in the knowledge of human limitations—a knowledge of which the "ideal husband" must have a good share.

RICHARD ELLMANN

Overtures to "Salome"

Salome, after having danced before the imaginations of European painters and sculptors for a thousand years, in the nineteenth century turned her beguilements to literature. Heine, Flaubert, Mallarmé, Huysmans, Laforgue and Wilde became her suitors. Jaded by exaltations of nature and of humanism, they inspected with something like relief a Biblical image of the *un*natural. Mario Praz, bluff, and skeptical of Salome's allurements, seeks to limit them by arguing that she became the type of no more than the *femme fatale*. By type he means, he says, something "like a neuralgic area. Some chronic ailment has created a zone of weakened resistance, and whenever an analogous phenomenon makes itself felt, it immediately confines itself to this predisposed area, until the process becomes a matter of mechanical monotony." But like most medical metaphors, this one doesn't apply easily to the arts, where repetition of subject is not a certain contra-indication to achievement. Most of these writers were conspicuous for their originality, and if they embraced so familiar a character from Biblical history, it was to accomplish effects they intended to make distinctive. As there are many Iseults, many Marys, so there were many Salomes, without monotony.

The fact that Wilde's *Salome* is a play, and a completed one, distinguishes it from other versions and helps to make it more original than Mr. Praz would have us believe. Mallarmé was not merely flattering when he congratulated Wilde on the "definitive evocation" of Salome, or when he took care to avoid seeming to copy Wilde when he returned to work on his own *Hérodiade*. Wilde's simple sentences and repeated words

From *Yearbook of Comparative and General Literature* 17 (1968), and *Tri-Quarterly*. Copyright © 1968 by *Yearbook of Comparative and General Literature* and *Tri-Quarterly*.

may indeed owe something to Maeterlinck or even (as a contemporary critic suggested) to Ollendorff—the Berlitz of that age—but they have become so habitual in modern drama as to seem anticipatory rather than derivative. The extreme concentration upon a single episode which is like an image, with a synchronized moon changing color from pale to blood-red in keeping with the action, and an atmosphere of frenzy framed in exotic chill, confirms Yeats's oblique acknowledgement that he had learned as much from Wilde as from the Noh drama for his dance plays. A torpid tetrarch (three Herods telescoped into one) lusting yet inert, a prophet clamoring from a well below the floorboards, are more congenial figures now that Beckett has accustomed us to paralysis, senile drivelling, voices from ashcans, and general thwart.

Mr. Praz, quick to deny Wilde any novelty, insists that the play's culminating moment, when Salome kisses the severed head of Iokanaan, is borrowed from Heine's *Atta Troll.* But in Heine's version kissing the head is a punishment after Herodias's death, not a *divertissement* before it, and the tone of caricature is quite unlike that of perverted horror which Wilde evokes. If some source has to be found—and it always has—I offer tentatively a dramatic poem called *Salome* published in Cambridge, Massachusetts, in 1862, by a young Harvard graduate named J. C. Heywood, and subsequently republished during the 1880s in London in the form of a trilogy. I have to admit that in Heywood as in Heine, it is Herodias, not Salome, who kisses the head, but at least she does so while still alive, and in a sufficiently grisly way. Wilde knew one part of Heywood's trilogy—he reviewed it in 1888, three years before writing his own play—and he may well have glanced at the other parts. Still, he isn't really dependent on Heywood either, since he exchanges mother for daughter and, unlike Heywood, makes this monstrous kissing the play's climax.

To read Heywood or other writers about Salome is to come to a greater admiration for Wilde's ingenuity. The general problem that I want to inquire into is what the play probably meant to Wilde and how he came to write it. Villainous women were not his usual subject, and even if they had been, there were others besides Salome he could have chosen. The reservoir of villainous women is always brimming. The choice of Salome would seem to inhere in her special relationship to John the Baptist and Herod. Sources offer little help in understanding this, and we have to turn to what might be called praeter-sources, elements which so pervaded Wilde's imaginative life as to become presences. Such a presence Amadis was for Don Quixote, or Vergil for Dante. In pursuing these I will offer no *explication de texte,* but what may well appear a divagation; perhaps to give it critical standing I should pronounce it *divagation,* though I hope to persuade you of its clandestine relevance. It includes, at any rate, those fugitive associations, often subliminal, which swarm beneath the fixed surface of the work, and which are as pertinent as is that surface to any study of the author's mind.

It will be necessary, therefore, to retrace certain of Wilde's close relationships. If Rilke is right in finding a few moments in a writer's life to be initiatory, then such an initiatory experience took place when Wilde left Ireland for England. He later said that the two turning-points in his life occurred "when my father sent me to Oxford, and when society sent me to prison." Wilde matriculated at Magdalen College, Oxford, on October 11, 1874, just before he was twenty. The two men he had most wanted to know at that time, he said, were Ruskin and Pater, both, conveniently enough, installed at the same place. He managed to meet Ruskin within a month, and though he didn't meet Pater so quickly, during his first three months at Oxford he made the acquaintance of Pater's *Studies in the History of the Renaissance*, which he soon called his "golden book," and subsequently referred to in a portentous phrase as "that book which has had such a strange influence over my life."

Three weeks after Wilde arrived, Ruskin gave a series of lectures on Florentine painting. During one of them he proposed to his students that, instead of developing their bodies in pointless games, in learning "to leap and to row, to hit a ball with a bat," they join him in improving the countryside. He proposed to turn a swampy lane near Ferry Hincksey into a flower-bordered country road. Such muscular effort would be ethical rather than narcissistic, medieval rather than classical. Although Oscar Wilde found rising at dawn more difficult than most men, he overcame his languor for Ruskin's sake. He would later brag comically that he had had the distinction of being allowed to fill "Mr. Ruskin's especial wheelbarrow" and even of being instructed by the master himself in the mysteries of wheeling such an object from place to place. At the end of term Ruskin was off to Venice, and Wilde could again lie late abed, comfortable in the thought that, as he said, "there was a long mound of earth across that swamp which a lively imagination might fancy was a road." The merely external signs of this noble enterprise soon sank from sight, but Wilde remembered it with affectionate respect, and his later insistence on functionalism in decoration and in women's dress, and on socialism based upon self-fulfillment in groups, were in the Ferry Hincksey tradition.

The road proved also to be the road to Ruskin. Wilde met his exalted foreman often during the ensuing years. In 1888, sending him a book, he summed up his feelings in this effusive tribute: "The dearest memories of my Oxford days are my walks and talks with you, and from you I learned nothing but what was good. How else could it be? There is in you something of prophet, of priest, and of poet, and to you the gods gave eloquence such as they have given to none other, so that your message might come to us with the fire of passion, and the marvel of music, making the deaf to hear, and the blind to see." That (like this prose) the prophet had weaknesses, made him if anything more prophetlike. Wilde was as aware of Ruskin's weaknesses as of his virtues. His letter of November 28, 1879, by which time he had taken his Oxford degree, mentions that he and Ruskin were going that night to see Henry Irving play Shylock, following which he himself was going on to the Millais ball. "How odd it is," Wilde remarks. The oddity lay not only in attending this particular play with the author of *The Stones of Venice,* but in proceeding afterwards to a ball which celebrated the marriage of John Everett Millais's daughter. Mrs. Millais had for six years been Mrs. Ruskin, and for three of those years Millais had been Ruskin's friend and protegé. The details of Ruskin's marriage and annulment were no doubt as well known at that time at Oxford by word of mouth as they have since become to us by dint of a dozen books. It was the fact that Ruskin and the Millaises did not speak to each other that obliged Wilde to leave Ruskin with Irving and proceed to the ball alone.

To call the Ruskin ambiance merely odd was Oxonian politeness. As soon as Ruskin was married, he explained to his wife that children would interfere with his work and impede necessary scholarly travel. Consummation might therefore wisely be deferred until later on, perhaps in six years' time when Effie would be twenty-five. Few of us here could claim an equal dedication to learning. In the meantime Effie need have no fear about the possible sinfulness of their restraint, since many early Christians lived in married celibacy all their lives. Effie tried to accommodate herself to this pedantic view, and Ruskin in turn was glad to oblige her on a lesser matter: that they go to live in Venice, since he was already planning to write a book about that city.

In Venice, while Ruskin sketched, Effie survived her boredom by going about with one or another of their friends. Ruskin encouraged her, perhaps (as she afterwards implied) too much. If he accompanied her to dances and masked balls, he often left early without her, having arranged that some gentleman friend escort her home. If she returned at 1:30 in the morning, he duly notified his parents in England, at the same time adding that he was completely at rest about her fidelity. Yet her obvious pleasure in pleasure, her flirtatiousness, her impatience with his studies, her delight in frivolity and late hours, struck Ruskin sometimes—however much he repudiated the outward thought—as forms of misconduct and disloyalty.

He said as much later. That Effie wasn't sexually unfaithful to him didn't of course prevent Ruskin, any more than it prevented Othello before him, from considering her so, or from transposing her mental dissonance into larger, vaguer forms of betrayal.

The Stones of Venice will always stand primarily as a work of art criticism. But criticism, as Wilde said, is the only civilized form of autobiography, and it is as a fragment—a large fragment—of Ruskin's autobiography that the book claims an added interest. In novels and poems we take for granted that some personal elements will be reflected, but in works of non-fiction we are more reluctant, and prefer to postulate an upper air of abstraction in which the dispassionate mind contemplates and orders materials that already have form and substance. Yet even the most impersonal of writers, Thucydides, writing about the fortunes of another city, shaped his events, as Cornford suggests, by preconceptions absorbed from Greek tragedy. Ruskin made no pretence of Thucydidean impersonality, and the influence of his reading of the Bible is manifest rather than latent. But some problems of his own life also were projected onto the Venetian scene. Rather than diminishing the book's value, they merge with its talent and add to its intensity.

It may be easier to be convinced that The Stones of Venice is in part autobiographical if we remember Ruskin's candid admission that Sesame and Lilies, a book he wrote a few years later, was a reflection of one particular experience. His preface expressly states that the section in it called "Lilies" was generated by his love for Rose La Touche. This love impelled him to idealize women, he says, even though "the chances of later life gave me opportunities of watching women in states of degradation and vindictiveness which opened to me the gloomiest secrets of Greek and Syrian tragedy. I have seen them betray their household charities to lust, their pledged love to devotion; I have seen mothers dutiful to their children, as Medea; and children dutiful to their parents, as the daughter of Herodias. . . ." His love for Rose La Touche also covertly leads him to quarrel in the book with pietism because Rose was that way inclined. The Stones of Venice deals less obviously, but with the same insistence, on the virtues and defects of the feminine character. As Ruskin remarks in Sesame and Lilies, "it has chanced to me, untowardly in some respects, fortunately in others (because it enables me to read history more clearly), to see the utmost evil that is in women. . . ." To Ruskin Venice is always she (to Mary McCarthy, invariably it), and the gender is not merely a form of speech but an image to be enforced in detail.

Accordingly Ruskin distinguishes two stages, with medieval Venice as virgin and Renaissance Venice as whore. The moment of transition is, apparently, the moment of copulation, and the moment of copulation is therefore (as in a familiar view of the Garden of Eden) the fall. When Ruskin describes the fallen state, he attributes to the city the very taste for masqued balls and merriment which he had ostentatiously tolerated in his wife. "She became in after times," he declares, "the revel of the earth, the masque of Italy: and *therefore* is she now desolate, but her glorious robe of gold and purple was given her when first she rose a vestal from the sea, not when she became drunk with the wine of her fornication." At the end of the first volume he again asserts, "It was when she wore the ephod of the priest, not the motley of the masquer, that the fire fell upon her from heaven. . . ." After that fire came another which changed the virgin city to its contrary: "Now Venice, as she was once the most religious, was in her fall the most corrupt, of European states; and as she was in her strength the centre of the pure currents of Christian architecture, so she is in her decline the source of the Renaissance. It was the originality and splendour of the Palaces of Vicenza and Venice which gave this school its eminence in the eyes of Europe; and the dying city, magnificent in her dissipation, and graceful in her follies, obtained wider worship in her decrepitude than in her youth, and sank from the midst of her admirers into her grave. Ruskin cannot bring himself to sketch out "the steps of her final ruin. That ancient curse was upon her, the curse of the cities of the plain, 'pride, fulness of bread, and abundance of idleness.' By the inner burning of her own passions, as fatal as the fiery reign of Gomorrah, she was consumed from her place among the nations, and her ashes are choking the channels of the dead salt sea." Just how passions should burn except inwardly may not be clear, especially since we can't suppose that Ruskin favored the translation of sensual thought into sensual action, but pride, gluttony, and sloth secure a more sinister confederate in the unnamable sin of lust, whose self-generated fire is contrasted with that fire which had earlier fallen on the city from heaven.

Ruskin's stridency shows how much he had this problem at heart. In fact, consummation and defilement were irrevocably united for him, in his life as in his criticism. The Renaissance (a new term then but already favorable in its connotations) was for him not a rebirth but a relapse. (In *De Profundis* Wilde accepted this view.) Ruskin's revulsion extended from coupling to begetting to having been begot. He had more trouble than most people in allowing that he was himself the product of his parents' intercourse. A small indication is to be found in an epitaph which he wrote for his mother (who already had an epitaph) long after her death, consecrating a memorial well, as he writes, "in memory of a maid's life as pure, and a mother's love as ceaseless. . . ." In Ruskin's mind his mother had immaculately passed from maid to mother without ever becoming a wife.

This singular epitaph may illuminate a point never adequately explained, why Ruskin dated the fall of Venice not only to an exact year, but to a specific day, May 8, 1418. His own explanation is that this was the deathday of the aged Venetian military leader Carlo Zeno, and he makes his usual citation of Pierre Daru's *Histoire de la République de Venise* as his authority. But Daru doesn't give Zeno's death such consequence. Ruskin might more easily, and more consistently with his own views, have taken the year 1423, when the old Doge Tommaso Mocenigo died and the new Doge, Foscari, began his less glorious rule. He is alone among writers on Venice in attaching this significance to Zeno's deathday, and in view of his known penchant for numerology the date invites attention. If Ruskin had been born exactly four hundred years after this date, in 1818, rather than in 1819, the choice might seem related to his theatrical self-laceration, as if to regret he had ever been born. But his terrors were for intercourse and conception rather than for birth. At the risk of impugning my own sanity as well as Ruskin's, I venture to propose that the date so carefully selected was, putatively, four hundred years to the day before his own conception—that act so impossible for him to meditate on with equanimity. That the moment of Venice's fall should be reiterated in the moment of his own begetting and be followed by his birth into an England only too ready (as he announces on the first page of his book) to fall—like a semi-detached Venice—anchored firmly the relationships Ruskin wished to dwell upon. In his parents' fall, as in that of our first parents, he saw the determination of an age's character and of his own.

Margaret Ruskin's marriage had made her a mother, while Effie Ruskin's "dissolute" behavior in Venice had made her—in fancy if not in fact—an adultress. Moral blame, from which his mother was freed, was shunted to his wife. Ruskin's own later summary of *The Stones of Venice* confirms that he had this theme in mind. In *The Crown of Wild Olive* (1866) he wrote, "*The Stones of Venice* had, from beginning to end, no other aim than to show that the Renaissance architecture of Venice had arisen out of, and in all its features indicated, a state of concealed national infidelity, and of domestic corruption." The trip to Scotland which Ruskin, his wife, and Millais took in 1853 strengthened the metaphors, and in later life he accused Millais of infidelity— artistic infidelity he called it—to the Pre-Raphaelite principles as Ruskin had earlier enunciated them. Venice, his wife, and his friend were all guilty of the same crime.

Necessary as Ruskin found it to think of himself as wronged, there were moments when he recognized his own culpability. After the annulment of his marriage he came, by a series of mental leaps, to try a revision of his character. In 1858, while looking at Veronese's "Solomon and Sheba" in Turin, he suddenly felt a wave of sympathy for the "strong and frank animality" of the greatest artists. He disavowed his earlier religious zeal, and became (though at the urging of his father and of Rose La Touche's mother he didn't publicly say so) quite skeptical. Then, as Wilenski points out, he began to acknowledge that his theory of history in *The Stones of Venice* was mistaken. Writing to Froude in 1864, he stated firmly, "There is no law of history any more than of a kaleidoscope. With certain bits of glass—shaken so, and so—you will get pretty figures, but what figures, Heaven only knows. . . . The wards of a Chubb's lock are infinite in their chances. Is the Key of Destiny made on a less complex principle?" This renunciation of historical law was intellectually daring, and emotionally as well, for it meant that he was trying to alter those "pretty figures" which earlier had enabled him to lock his own conception and marriage into the history of Venice. As part of this change, he resolved to propose marriage to Rose La Touche, and in 1866 he at last did so. Rose La Touche, no mean calendar-watcher herself, said she could not answer for two years, or perhaps for four. Ruskin abided by her verdict with desperation; his diary records the passing of not only these anniversaries but, since she died soon after, of year after year following her death. No one will mock Ruskin's pain, or his struggle to overcome his fears and become as animal as Veronese.

Rose La Touche had been dead less than a year when Ruskin and Wilde met and took walks together. Neither professor nor pupil was reticent, and Wilde probably divined the matters that Ruskin was unwilling to confide. At any rate, the moral law as imparted by Ruskin, even with the softenings he now wished to introduce, was for Wilde sublime—and berserk. In Ruskin, whom everyone called a prophet, the ethical life was noble and yet, in its weird chastity, perverse. Against its rigors life offered an antidote, and what life was had been articulated by Pater, who saw it not in terms of stones but of waters, not of monuments but of rivery passions. Pater was like Wilde in that, at the same age of nineteen, he too had fallen under Ruskin's sway. He soon broke free, his conscience unclenched itself. He surprised a devout friend by nonetheless attempting, although he had lost his faith, to take orders in the Anglican Church. His friend complained to the bishop and scotched this diabolic ordination. The *Studies in the History of the Renaissance*, Pater's first book, doesn't mention Ruskin by name, but uses him throughout as an adversary. Pater's view of the Renaissance did not differ in being more detached; in its way it was just as personal, and it ended in a secular sermon which ran exactly counter to that of *The Stones of Venice.* It is Ruskin inverted. Pater is all blend where Ruskin is all severance. He calls superficial Ruskin's view that the Renaissance was "a fashion which set in at a definite period." For Pater it was rather "an uninterrupted effort of the middle age." One age was older, one younger, they encountered each other like lovers.

An atmosphere of suppressed invitation runs through Pater's book as an atmosphere of suppressed refusal runs through Ruskin's. The first essay of *Studies in the . . . Renaissance* recounts at length how the friendship of Amis and Amile (in the thirteenth-century story) was so full and intense that they were buried together rather than with their respective wives. Later essays dwell with feeling upon such encounters as that of young Pico della Mirandola, looking like a Phidian statue, with the older Ficino, or as that—planned but prevented by murder—of Winckelmann and the still callow Goethe. For Ruskin the Renaissance is an aged Jezebel, while for Pater it is a young man, his hair wreathed in roses more than in thorns, such a youth as Leonardo painted as John the Baptist. In describing this painting, Pater lingers to point out that the saint's body doesn't look as if it had come from a wilderness, and he finds John's smile intriguingly treacherous and suggestive of a good deal—which may be Victorian hinting at the heresy, a specially homosexual one, that Christ and John (not to mention Leonardo and his model) were lovers.

Whatever Ruskin says about strength and weakness, Pater opposes. The decay against which *The Stones of Venice* fulminates is for Pater "the fascination of corruption," and images of baleful female power, such as Leonardo's Medusa and other "daughters of Herodias," are discovered to be "clairvoyant" and "electric," when Ruskin had found the daughter of Herodias monstrously degraded. Instead of praising the principle of *Noli me tangere*, so ardently espoused by Ruskin, Pater objects to Christian asceticism that it "discredits the slightest sense of touch." Ruskin had denounced "ripe" ornamentation in terms which evoked elements of the adult female body: "I mean," he said, "that character of extravagance in the ornament itself which shows that it was addressed to jaded faculties; a violence and coarseness in curvature, a depth of shadow, a lusciousness in arrangement of line, evidently arising out of an incapability of feeling the true beauty of chaste forms and restrained power. I do not know any character of design which may be more easily recognized at a glance than this over-lusciousness. . . . We speak loosely and inaccurately of 'overcharged' ornament, with an obscure feeling that there is indeed something in visible Form which is correspondent to Intemperance in moral habits. . . ." But for Pater overcharged ornament is rather an "overwrought delicacy, almost of wantonness," or "a languid Eastern deliciousness."

Ruskin strenuously combatted what he considered to be a false fusion of classicism and Christianity in the Renaissance. "It would have been better," he said, "to have worshipped Diana and Jupiter at once than have gone through life naming one God, imagining another, and dreading none." Galleries had no business placing Aphrodite and the Madonna, a Bacchanal and a Nativity, side by side. But this juxtaposition was exactly what Pater endorsed. For him European culture was what he called, following Hegel to some extent, a synthesis. To countervail Ruskin's diptych of Venice as virgin of the Adriatic and whore of Babylon, he offered as his Renaissance altarpiece the Mona Lisa of Leonardo. His famous description begins, "The presence that rose beside the waters," and it is clear that he is summoning up not only Lisa, but Venus rising like Ruskin's favorite city from the sea. Lisa has, according to this gospel of Saint Walter, mothered both Mary and Helen, exactly the indiscriminateness, as well as the fecundity, which Ruskin condemned. Pater's heroine, as Salvador Dali has implied by giving her a moustache more suited to Pater, is an androgyne: the activities attributed to her, dealing with foreign merchants and diving in deep seas, seem more male than female. She blends the sexes, she combines sacred and profane. Like Saint John, she has about her something of the Borgias.

Against Ruskin's insistence upon innocence, Pater proffers what he bathetically terms, in the suppressed and then altered and reinstated conclusion to the *Renaissance*, "great experiences." He urges his readers to seek out high passions, only being sure they are passions; later, only being sure they are high. The Renaissance is for him the playtime of sensation, even its spiritual aspects being studies in forms of sensation. W. H. Mallock parodied this aspect by having Pater, as the effete "Mr. Rose" in *The New Republic*, lust for a pornographic book. Something of the extraordinary effect of Pater's *Renaissance* comes from its being exercises in the seduction of young men by the wiles of culture. And yet Pater may not have seduced them in any way except stylistically. When Wilde presented Lord Alfred Douglas to him, the flagrancy of the homosexual relationship was probably, as Lawrence Evans suggests, the cause of the rift between Pater and Wilde which then developed.

Pater and Ruskin were for Wilde at first imagined, and then actual figures; then they came to stand heraldically, burning unicorn and uninflamed satyr, in front of two portals of his mental theatre. He sometimes allowed them to battle, at other times tried to reconcile them. A good example is his first long published work. This was an ambitious review of the paintings in a new London gallery; he wrote it in 1877, his third year at Oxford, for the *Dublin University Magazine*. The article takes the form of a rove through the three rooms, which had been done, Wilde said admiringly, "in scarlet damask above a dado of dull green and gold." (Ruskin, who also attended, complained that this décor was "dull in itself" and altogether unsuited to the pictures.) Upon entering, Wilde immediately belauds Burne-Jones and Hunt as "the greatest masters of colour that we have ever had in England, with the single exception of Turner"—a compliment to Ruskin's advocacy of Turner and to the sponsorship of the Pre-Raphaelites by both Ruskin and Pater. Wilde then, to praise Burne-Jones further, quotes Pater's remark that for Botticelli natural things "have a spirit upon them by which they become expressive to the spirit," and as he sweeps through the gallery he finds occasion to savor the same sweet phrase again. He also manages to mention the portrait of Ruskin by Millais, though it was not on exhibition. Reaching the end, he salutes "that revival of culture and love of beauty which in great part owes its birth to Mr. Ruskin, and which Mr. Swinburne and Mr. Pater and Mr. Symons and Mr. Morris and many others are fostering and keeping alive, each in his peculiar fashion." He slipped another quotation from Pater into this final paragraph, but a watchful editor slipped it out again.

Wilde's review of the exhibition is not so interesting as Ruskin's, in *Fors Clavigera* 79, which roused Millais to fury and Whistler to litigation. But it did result in Wilde's finally meeting Pater who, having been sent a copy of the review, invited him to call. Their subsequent friendship afforded Wilde a chance to study the student of the Renaissance. He did not lose his admiration, as we can surmise from the poem "Hélas!" which he wrote a little later. In it he invokes both of his mentors as if they were contrary forces tugging at him. After owning up to frivolity, Wilde says,

> Surely there was a time I might have trod
> The august heights, and from life's dissonance
> Struck one clear chord to reach the ears of God.

The chief reference is to Gothic architecture, celebrated by Ruskin because, though fraught with human imperfection—"life's dissonance"—it reached towards heaven. In the next lines Wilde confesses to having fallen away a little:

> Is that time dead? Lo, with a little rod,
> I did but touch the honey of romance.
> And must I lose a soul's inheritance?

Here he is quoting Jonathan's remark to Saul, "I did but taste a little honey with the end of the rod that was in mine hand, and lo! I must die," which Wilde remembered Pater's having conspicuously quoted and interpreted in the *Renaissance* in his essay on Winckelmann. For Pater Jonathan's remark epitomizes "the artistic life, with its inevitable sensuousness," and is contrasted with Christian asceticism and its antagonism to touch. If the taste for honey is a little decadent, then so much the better. Wilde is less sanguine about this appetite here. But as Jonathan was saved, so Wilde, for all his alases, expected to be saved too, partly because he had never renounced the Ruskin conscience, only foregone it for a time.

The tutelary presences of Pater and Ruskin survived in Wilde's more mature writings. In *The Picture of Dorian Gray*, for example, Pater is enclosed (like an unhappy dryad caught in a tree trunk) in Lord Henry Wotton. Lord Henry's chief sin is quoting without acknowledgment from the *Renaissance*. He tells Dorian, as Pater told Mona Lisa, "You have drunk deeply of everything . . . and it has all been to you no more than the sound of music." He predicts, against the "curious revival of Puritanism" (a cut at Ruskin) a new hedonism, the aim of which will be "experience itself, and not the fruits of experience." It will "teach man to concentrate himself upon the moments of a life that is but a moment." These are obvious tags from the Conclusion to the *Renaissance*. Lord Henry's advice to Dorian, "Let nothing be lost upon you. Be always searching for new sensations," was so closely borrowed from the same essay that Pater, who wrote a review of the book, was at great pains to distinguish Lord Henry's philosophy from his own. Wilde seems to have intended not to distinguish them, however, and to offer (through the disastrous effects of Lord Henry's influence upon Dorian) a criticism of Pater.

As for Ruskin, his presence in the book is more tangential. The painter Hallward has little of Ruskin at the beginning, but gradually he moves closer to that pillar of esthetic taste and moral judgment upon which Wilde leaned, and after Hallward is safely murdered, Dorian with sudden fondness recollects a trip they had made to Venice together, when his friend was captivated by Tintoretto's art. Ruskin was of course the English discoverer and champion of Tintoretto, so that the allusion is specific. The ending of *Dorian Gray* executes a Ruskinesque repudiation of a Pateresque career of self-gratifying sensations. Wilde defined the moral in so witty a way as to content neither of his mentors: in letters to newspapers he said *Dorian Gray* showed that "all excess, as well as all renunciation, brings its own punishment." Not only are Hallward and Dorian punished by death, but, Wilde asserted, Lord Henry is punished too. Lord Henry's offense was in seeking "to be merely the spectator of life. He finds that those who reject the battle are more deeply wounded than those who take part in it." The phrase "spectator of life" was one that Wilde used in objecting to Pater's *Marius the Epicurean*. However incongruous his conception of himself as activist, with it he lorded it over his too donnish friend. For Pater, while he touted (sporadically at least) the life of pleasure, was careful not to be caught living it. He idealized touch until it became contemplation. He allowed only his eye to participate in the high passions about which he loved to expatiate. Dorian at least had the courage to risk himself.

In *Dorian Gray* the Pater side of Wilde's thought is routed, though not deprived of fascination. Yet Hallward, when his ethical insistence brings him close to Ruskin, is killed too. In *The Soul of Man under Socialism*, also written in 1891, Wilde superimposes Ruskin's social ethic upon Pater's "full expression of personality," fusing instead of destroying them. In *Salome*, to which I come at last, the formulation is close to *Dorian Gray*, with both opposites executed. Behind the figure of Iokanaan lurks the image of that perversely untouching, untouchable prophet John whom Wilde knew at Oxford. When Iokanaan, up from his cistern for a moment, cries to Salome, "Arrière, fille de Sodome! Ne me touchez pas. Il ne faut pas profaner le temple du Seigneur Dieu," a thought of Ruskin, by now sunk down into madness, can scarcely have failed to cross Wilde's mind. By this time Wilde would also have recognized in the prophet's behavior (as in Ruskin's) something of his own, for after his first three years of marriage he had discontinued sexual relations with his wife. Iokanaan is not Ruskin, but he is Ruskinism as Wilde understood that pole of his character. Then when Salome evinces her appetite for strange experiences, her eagerness to kiss a literally disembodied lover in a relation at once totally sensual and totally "mystical" (Wilde's own term for her), she shows something of that diseased contemplation for which Wilde had reprehended Pater. Her adaptation, or perversion, of the Song of Songs to describe a man's rather than a woman's beauty also is reminiscent of Pater's *Renaissance* as well as of Wilde's predisposition. It is Salome, and not Pater, who dances the dance of the seven veils, but her virginal yet perverse sensuality is related to Paterism.

Admittedly the play takes place in Judea and not in Oxford. Wilde wanted the play to have meaning outside his own psychodrama. Yet Wilde's tutelary voices from the university, now fully identified as forces within himself, seem to be in attendance, clamoring for domination. Both Iokanaan and Salome are executed, however, and at the command of the tetrarch. The execution of Salome was not in the Bible, but Wilde insisted upon it. So at the play's end the emphasis shifts suddenly to Herod, who is seen to have yielded to Salome's sensuality, and then to the moral revulsion of Iokanaan from that sensuality, and to have survived them both. In Herod Wilde was suggesting that *tertium quid* which he felt to be his own nature, susceptible to contrary impulses but not abandoned for long to either.

Aubrey Beardsley divined the autobiographical element in Herod, and in one of his illustrations gave the tetrarch the author's face. Herod speaks like Wilde in purple passages about peacocks or in such an epigram as, "Il ne faut pas regarder que dans les miroirs. Car les miroirs ne nous montrent que les masques." Just what Wilde thought his own character to be, as distinct from the alternating forces of Pater and Ruskin, is implied in a remark he made in 1883 to George Woodberry, who promptly relayed it to Charles Eliot Norton. Wilde told Woodberry that Ruskin "like Christ bears the sins of the world, but that he himself was 'always like Pilate, washing his hands of all responsibility.' " Pilate in the story of Christ occupies much the same role as Herod in the story of John the Baptist. In other letters Wilde continues to lament his own weakness, yet with so much attention as to imply that it may have a certain fibre to it. In March 1877 he wrote, "I shift with every breath of thought and am weaker and more self-deceiving than ever," and in 1886 he remarked, "Sometimes I think that the artistic life is a long and lovely suicide, and am not sorry that it is so." What he more and more held against both his mentors was a vice they shared equally, that of narrowness. To keep to any one form of life is limiting, he said in De Profundis, and added without remorse, "I had to pass on."

Herod too passes on, strong in his tremblings, a leaf but a sinuous one, swept but not destroyed by successive waves of spiritual and physical passion, in possession of what Wilde in a letter calls "a curious mixture of ardour and of indifference. I myself would sacrifice everything for a new experience, and I know there is no such thing as a new experience at all . . . I would go to the stake for a sensation and be a sceptic to the last!" Here too there are martyrdom and abandonment, with a legal right to choose and yet stay aloof. Proust had something of the same idea when he said of Whistler's quarrel with Ruskin that both men were right. In that same reconciling vein Wilde in De Profundis celebrates Christ as an artist, and the artist as Christ. And in Wilde's last play, when Jack declares at the end, "I've now realized for the first time in my life the vital Importance of Being Earnest," he is demonstrating again that Ruskin's earnestness, and Pater's paraded passionateness, are for the artist not mutually exclusive but may, by wit, by weakness, by self-withholding, be artistically, as well as tetrarchically, compounded.

RICHARD ELLMANN

The Critic as Artist as Wilde

Wilde is the one writer of the Nineties whom everyone still reads, or more precisely, has read. The mixture of frivolity and pathos in his career continues to arrest us. That career displays its self-conjugation in Wilde's own terms of "The Critic as Artist."

In 1914 Henry James could complain that there was not enough criticism about to give novelists their bearings, while T. S. Eliot and Saul Bellow have since regretted, for different reasons and in different tones of voice, that there is now too much. The obtrusive place of the critic today can be related to a methodological emphasis which is conspicuous in other disciplines as well. But Wilde was one of the first to see that the exaltation of the artist required a concomitant exaltation of the critic. If art was to have a special train, the critic must keep some seats reserved on it.

Wilde reached this conclusion by way of two others. The first is that criticism plays a vital role in the creative process. If this sounds like T. S. Eliot admonishing Matthew Arnold, Wilde had expressed it, also as an admonition to Arnold, almost thirty years before. The second is that criticism is an independent branch of literature with its own procedures. "I am always amused," says Wilde, "by the silly vanity of those writers and artists of our day who seem to imagine that the primary function of the critic is to chatter about their second-rate work." And he complains that "The poor reviewers are apparently reduced to be the reporters of the police-court of literature, the chroniclers of the doings of the habitual criminals of art." In protesting the independence of criticism, Wilde sounds like an ancestral Northrop Frye or Roland Barthes. These portentous comparisons do indeed claim virtue by association, and such claims may be broadened. André Gide found Nietzsche less exciting because he had read Wilde, and Thomas Mann in one of his last essays remarks almost with chagrin on how many of Nietzsche's aphorisms might have been expressed by Wilde, and how many of Wilde's by Nietzsche. What I think can be urged for Wilde then, is that for his own reasons and in his own way he laid the basis for many critical positions which are still debated in much the same terms, and which we like to attribute to more ponderous names.

When Wilde formulated his theories the public was more hostile to criticism than it is now, and Wilde was flaunting his iconoclasm, his contempt for the unconsidered and so uncritical pieties of his age. This in fact was his mode: not to speak for the Victorians, or for the prematurely old writers who dithered that they were the end of an era, as if they must expire with the 1800s. Wilde proposed to speak for the young, with even excessive eagerness. His own age was always a little embarrassing for him, because he had already spent three years at Trinity College, Dublin, when he went up to Oxford. He was not above a little deception on this score. In 1877, when he was twenty-three, he sent a poem to Gladstone with a letter saying, "I am little more than a boy." And in a poem written that year he spoke of his "boyish passion" and described himself as "one who scarce has seen some twenty summers." This line, in turn, he repeated in his poem "The Sphinx," finished when he was forty. Even in court he injudiciously testified he was two years younger than he was, so that he sounds a little like Falstaff shouting to Bardolph during the robbery, "They hate us youth." Wilde's mode was calculated juvenescence, and the characters in his books are always being warned by shrewder characters of the danger of listening to people older than themselves. To help reduce that danger, Wilde's characters are invariably parentless. The closest kin allowed is an aunt.

Like Stendhal, Wilde thought of himself as a voice of the age to be, rather than of the one that was fading. Yet like anyone else writing criticism in the nineteenth century, he had to come to terms with the age that had been, and especially with everybody's parent, Matthew Arnold. Wilde sought Arnold's approbation for his first book, *Poems*, in 1881, which he sent with a letter stressing their shared Oxonian connections. These extended, though he wisely did not enforce the claim, to their both having won the Newdigate. Actually their prize-winning poems offer a contrast of manners, Arnold's being just as determined to appear older as Wilde's younger than his years. Arnold replied politely.

But by 1881 Arnold was genuinely old, and seven years later, in

1888 he was dead. Wilde's only book of criticism, *Intentions*, was written during the three years following Arnold's death and published in 1891, as if to take over that critical burden and express what Arnold had failed to say. Yeats thought the book "wonderful" and Walter Pater handsomely praised it for carrying on, "more perhaps than any other writer, the brilliant critical work of Matthew Arnold." Pater's encomium is a reminder, however, not to ignore *him*. There are not two but three critical phases in the late nineteenth century, with Pater transitional between Arnold and Wilde.

In 1864, lecturing from the Oxford Chair of Poetry on "The Function of Criticism at the Present Time," Arnold declared—to everyone's lasting memory—that the "aim of criticism is to see the object as in itself it really is." This statement went with his demand for "disinterested curiosity" as the mark of the critic; its inadvertent effect was to put the critic on his knees before the work he was discussing. Not everyone enjoyed this position. Nine years later Walter Pater wrote his preface to *Studies in the History of the Renaissance*. Pretending to agree with Arnold's definition of the aim of criticism, he quoted it, then added, "the first step towards seeing one's object as it really is, is to know one's impression as it really is, to discriminate it, to realise it distinctly." But Pater's corollary subtly altered the original proposition; it shifted the center of attention from the rock of the object to the winds of the perceiver's sensations. It made the critic's own work more important as well as more subjective. If observation is still the word, the critic looks within himself as often as out upon the object.

Wilde had been Pater's disciple, and in *Intentions* eighteen years later he tweaks Arnold's nose with the essay which in its first published form was entitled, "The True Function and Value of Criticism: with Some Remarks on the Importance of Doing Nothing." Here Wilde rounded on Arnold by asserting that the aim of criticism is to see the object as it really is not. This aim might seem to justify the highly personal criticism of Ruskin and Pater, and Wilde uses them as examples; his contention goes beyond their practice, however; he wishes to free critics from subordination, to grant them a larger share in the production of literature. While he does not forbid them to explain a book, they might prefer, he said, to deepen a book's mystery. (This purpose is amusing but out of date now; who could deepen the mystery of *Finnegans Wake*?) At any rate, their context would be different from that of the creative artist. For just as the artist claimed independence of received experience (Picasso tells us that art is "what nature is not"), so the critic claimed independence of received books. "The highest criticism," according to Wilde, "is the record of one's own soul." More closely he explained that the critic must have all literature in his mind and see particular works in that perspective rather than in isolation. Thus he, and we as well,

> shall be able to realise, not merely our own lives, but the collective spirit of the race, and so to make ourselves absolutely modern, in the true meaning of the word modernity. For he to whom the present is the only thing that is present, knows nothing of the age in which he lives. To realise the nineteenth century, one must realise every century that has preceded it and that has contributed to its making.

Through knowledge the critic might become more creative than the creative artist, a paradox which has been expressed with more solemnity by Norman Podhoretz about literature of the present day.

Wilde reached these formulations of his aesthetic ideas late in his short life. They were latent, however, in his earliest known essay, "The Rise of Historical Criticism," which he wrote as a university exercise. While praising historians for their scrupulousness, Wilde finds the core of history to be the wish not merely to paint a picture, but to investigate laws and tendencies. He celebrates those historians who impose dominion upon fact instead of surrendering to it. Later he was to say much more boldly, "The one duty we owe to history is to rewrite it," and to praise Herodotus as father not of history but of lies. It is part of his larger conception that the one duty (or better, whim) we owe nature, reality, or the world, is to reconstruct it.

When Wilde turned to literary as distinguished from historical criticism, he at first was content to follow Pater. Wilde was won by Pater's espousal of gemlike flames and of high temperatures both in words and in life. Next to him Arnold sounded chilly, never so Victorian as when he was cogently criticizing Victorianism. That word "impression," with which Pater sought to unlock everything, became a favorite word in both Wilde and later in Arthur Symons, and was only arrested by Yeats in the late 1890s because he could not bear so much impermanence and insisted on a metaphysical basis—the *Anima Mundi*—for transitory moods. Like the word "absurd" today, though without a systematic philosophy behind it, the word "impression" agitated against pat assumptions and preconceptions.

Pater's vocabulary shapes the initial poem of Wilde's book of verse, published when he was twenty-five. This poem "Hélas!" encapsulates much of Wilde's temperament, but with Pater's coloring:

> To drift with every passion till my soul
> Is a stringed lute on which all winds can play,
> Is it for this that I have given away

Mine ancient wisdom, and austere control?
Methinks my life is a twice-written scroll
Scrawled over on some boyish holiday
With idle songs for pipe and virelay
Which do but mar the secret of the whole.
Surely there was a time I might have trod
The sunlit heights, and from life's dissonance
Struck one clear chord to reach the ears of God:
Is that time dead? lo! with a little rod
I did but touch the honey of romance—
And must I lose a soul's inheritance?

To call the poem "Hélas!," to sigh in a foreign language, alerts us that the confession to follow will luxuriate in its penitence. The Biblical archaisms which occur later offer compunction suitably perfumed. "To drift" may well put us off as weak; on the other hand, "to drift with every passion" is not so bad. As its image of passivity, the poem offers "a stringed lute on which all winds can play." For the romantics the Aeolian harp was a favorable image because it harmonized man and nature. Here the winds are winds of temptation, rather than gusts of Lake Country air. The rhetorical question which begins, "Is it for this?" sounds reproachful enough, yet the phrases "ancient wisdom" and "austere control"—self-congratulatory since Wilde never had either—are so vague as to constitute a stately but equally unenergetic alternative to drifting.

The word "drift" comes down from Oxford in the 1870s. It occupies a prominent position in Pater's *Studies in the History of the Renaissance*, and specifically in the notorious conclusion to that book. This "Conclusion" was included in the edition of 1873, but omitted in 1877, when Wilde was at Oxford, on the ground that it "might possibly mislead" the young, who accordingly thronged to be misled by the first edition. It was the boldest thing Pater ever wrote; he drew upon the scientific work of his day to deny the integrity of objects. Physical life is now recognized, he says, to be a concurrence of forces rather than a group of things; the mind has no fixities either. He hits upon a metaphor of liquidity such as William James and Bergson were to adopt a little later in characterizing consciousness as a river or stream; Pater says more balefully that consciousness is a whirlpool, an image which later both Yeats and Pound relished. In our physical life, Pater grants, we sometimes feel momentarily at rest; in our consciousness, however, altering the whirlpool image, he finds "nothing but the race of the mid-stream, a drift of momentary acts of sight and passion and thought." To drift is not so wanton, then, as inevitable. To guide our drifting we should rely not on sights or thoughts, in Pater's view, but on "great passions." "Only be sure it is passion," he puts in as a caveat. He urges his readers to recognize that "not the fruit of experience, but experience itself, is the goal." "Our one hope lies in getting as many pulsations as possible into the given time." This attempt to render experience in terms of quantitatively measurable pulsations sounds a little like *Principles of Literary Criticism*, but Pater's tone is not like Richards'; he plays on the flute for the young to follow him.

When Pater at last decided to reprint this "Conclusion" (in 1888), he toned it down a little. In *Marius the Epicurean* (1885), also later, the word "drift" is again prominent, but this time is pejorative instead of merely descriptive. To suit his later and more decorous manner, Pater, in reviewing *Dorian Gray*, complained of the book's "dainty Epicurean theory" because, he said:

> A true Epicureanism aims at a complete though harmonious development of man's entire organism. To lose the moral sense therefore, for instance, the sense of sin and righteousness . . . is to lose, or lower, organisation, to become less complex, to pass from a higher to a lower degree of development.

The letting-go, as well as the drawing-back, of Pater are both evident in Wilde; his work celebrates both impulses, balancing or disporting with them. In a letter of March 1887, written four years before "Hélas!," he informs an Oxford friend:

> I have got rather keen on Masonry lately and believe in it awfully—in fact would be awfully sorry to have to give it up in case I secede from the Protestant Heresy. I now breakfast with Father Parkinson, go to St Aloysius, talk sentimental religion to Dunlop and altogether am caught in the fowler's snare, in the wiles of the Scarlet Woman—I may go over in the vac. I have dreams of a visit to Newman, of the holy sacrament in a new Church, and of a quiet and peace afterwards in my soul. I need not say, though, that I shift with every breath of thought and am weaker and more self-deceiving than ever.
>
> If I *could hope* that the Church would wake in me some earnestness and purity I would go over *as a luxury*, if for no better reasons. But I can hardly hope it would, and to go over to Rome would be to sacrifice and give up my two great gods "Money and Ambition."

In this letter Wilde testifies playfully to the same yearning to be earnest that he shows in "Hélas!" and then mocks in his later comedy. He is half-converted to Catholicism, half to Masonry—that these two groups cannot bear each other does not prevent their being equally attractive to him; they have parity as new areas of sensation, to be enjoyed willfully and passingly. If, as Wilde announced later, "the best way to resist temptation is to yield to it," the reason is that having done so, one may pass on to the next and the next, and in this concourse one may keep a residual freedom by not lingering with any single temptation long.

During the four years between writing this letter and writing "Hélas!," Wilde had put aside both Catholicism and Masonry. In his sonnet he has in mind chiefly his formal education as contrasted with his romantic self-indulgence. A classicist by training, Wilde considered Hellenism to be the more basic side of his nature, overlaid, but only as a palimpsest conceals the original, by a more modern mode. He berates himself, gently. His new life is made up of "idle songs for pipe and virelay," a self-accusation which only concedes frivolity, not depravity. Moreover, it is artistic frivolity, a further mitigation. Wilde remembered Pater's comment in the same "Conclusion" that "the wisest" instead of living spend their lives in "art and song." If it is wrong to drift, and Wilde hedges a little, then it is less wrong to drift gracefully. A "boyish holiday" is also not the most offensive way to spend one's time, especially if one likes boys.

The sestet of the poem restates the issue, with new dashes of metaphor. The poet then asks histrionically, "Is that time dead?" He won't say for sure, but again he sweetens his offense: he has but touched with Jonathan's rod the honey of romance. The last question is not so much despairing as hopeful. Wilde felt he was superior to both classical and romantic modes, because he could manipulate both: he said in his essay on the English renaissance that this variability was the strength of the new movement in letters to which he belonged. He thought he had physiological as well as artistic support for his method, because "the desire of any very intensified emotion [is] to be relieved by some emotion that is its opposite." He shifts therefore from foot to foot in other poems besides "Hélas!" "The Sphinx" begins with a fascinated invocation of the sphinx and ends with a strident rejection of her. Wilde summarizes his state or rather his flow of mind in a letter:

> Sometime you will find, even as I have found, that there is no such thing as a romantic experience; there are romantic memories, and there is the desire of romance—that is all. Our most fiery moments of ecstasy are merely shadows of what somewhere else we have felt, or of what we long some day to feel. So at least it seems to me. And, strangely enough, what comes of all this is a curious mixture of ardour and of indifference. I myself would sacrifice everything for a new experience, and I know there is no such thing as a new experience at all. I think I would more readily die for what I do not believe in than for what I hold to be true. I would go to the stake for a sensation and be a sceptic to the last! Only one thing remains infinitely fascinating to me, the mystery of moods. To be master

of these moods is exquisite, to be mastered by them more exquisite still. Sometimes I think that the artistic life is a long and lovely suicide, and am not sorry that it is so.

Life then is a willed deliquescence, or more exactly, a progressive surrender of the self to all the temptations appropriate to it.

What Wilde needed was not to avoid the precious occasions of evil in "Hélas!" but to approach more enterprising ones. Yet after his *Poems* appeared in 1881 he was at check for almost six years. He kept busy; he went on a lecture tour for a whole year to America; he returned to England and went lecturing on; he tried unsuccessfully for a post as school inspector such as Matthew Arnold had; erratically still, he married in 1884 and took up husbanding, begetting two children born in 1885 and 1886. Then in 1887 Wilde began the publications by which he is known. He wrote a volume of stories, and one of fairy tales, then one of criticism, then five plays, besides editing from 1887 to 1889 a magazine, *Woman's World*—a patrician equivalent of the A & P *Woman's Day*. It would seem that something roused him from the pseudo-consolidation of marriage and lectures, which were dilettantism for him, to genuine consolidation which seemed dilettantism to others.

This something appears in the original version of *The Picture of Dorian Gray*, published in *Lippincott's Magazine*. Wilde emphasizes more there than in the final version the murder of the painter Basil Hallward by Dorian; it is the turning-point in Dorian's experience, a plunge from insinuations of criminal tendency to crime itself. The murder at once protects the secret of his double life and vents his revulsion against the man who wants him innocent still. In *Lippincott's* Wilde specifies: "It was on the 7th of November, the eve of his own thirty-second birthday, as he often remembered afterwards. . . ." Then when the novel was published as a book, Wilde altered this date: "It was on the ninth of November, the eve of his own thirty-eighth birthday, as he often remembered afterwards."

Altering Dorian's age would be gratuitous if Wilde had not attached significance to his own thirty-second year which began in 1886. The passage must have been autobiographical, and such a conjecture receives support from Robert Ross, who boasted that it was he, at the age of seventeen, who in 1886 first seduced Wilde to homosexual practices. Wilde evidently considered this sudden alteration of his life a pivotal matter, to be recast as Dorian's murder of Hallward. He himself moved from pasteboard marriage to the expression of long latent proclivities, at some remove from the "ancient wisdom" and "austere control" to which he had earlier laid claim as his basic nature. Respectability, always an enemy, was destroyed in his own house. The first work which came out of the new Wilde was, appropriately, "Lord Arthur Savile's Crime," in which murder is comically enacted and successfully concealed.

From late in the year 1886 then, Wilde was able to think of himself, if he wanted to, as criminal. Up to that time he could always consider himself an innocent misunderstood; now he lived in such a way as to confirm suspicions. Instead of challenging Victorian society only by words, he acted in such a way as to create scandal. Indiscreet by nature, he was indiscreet also by conviction, and he waged his war somewhat openly. He sensed that his new life was a source of literary effect. As he wrote later of Thomas Wainewright: "His crimes seem to have had an important effect upon his art. They gave a strong personality to his style, a quality that his early work certainly lacked." He returned to this idea: "One can fancy an intense personality being created out of sin," and in "The Soul of Man Under Socialism," he thought that "Crime . . . under certain conditions, may be said to have created individualism." In "The Portrait of Mr W. H." (1889), he made Shakespeare's sonnets depend upon a similarly forbidden love affair, with an actor the same age as Ross. Thomas Mann's Mario Kröger speaks of a banker who discovers his literary talent by committing a serious crime for which he is put in prison. The artist-criminal is implicit in romantic and symbolistic theories of art, but Wilde anticipates the explicitness on this subject of both Mann and Gide, as he does that of Cavafy in "Their Beginning" or of Auden in *About the House:*

> Time has taught you
> > how much inspiration
> your vices brought you. . . .

Wilde might have discounted the sinfulness of his conduct and applied to himself his own epigram: "Wickedness is a myth invented by good people to account for the curious attractiveness of others." But he was quite content to think of himself as sinful.

He now succeeded in relating his new discoveries about himself to aesthetic theory. His only formal book of criticism, *Intentions,* has the same secret spring as his later plays and stories. Ostensibly he generally says that the spheres of art and of ethics are absolutely distinct and separate. But occasionally, overtly or covertly, he states that for the artist crime does pay, by instilling itself in his content and affecting his form. Each of the four essays that make up *Intentions* is to some degree subversive, as if to demonstrate that the intentions of the artist are not strictly honorable. The first and the last, "The Decay of Lying" and "The Truth of Masks," celebrate art for rejecting truths, faces, and all that paraphernalia in favor of lies and masks. Wilde doesn't do this in the romantic way of extolling the imagination, for while he uses that word he is a little chary of it; the imagination is itself too natural, too involuntary, for his view of art. He prefers lying because it sounds more willful, because it is no outpouring of the self, but a conscious effort to mislead. "All fine imaginative work," Wilde affirms, "is self-conscious and deliberate. A great poet sings because he chooses to sing." On the other hand, "if one tells the truth, one is sure, sooner or later, to be found out!" "All bad poetry springs from genuine feeling." Wilde celebrates art not in the name of Ariel, as the romantics would, but in the name of Ananias.

He finds art to have two basic energies, both of them subversive. One asserts its magnificent isolation from experience, its unreality, its sterility. He would concur with Nabokov that art is a kind of trick played on nature, an *illicit* creation by man. "All art is entirely useless," Wilde declares. "Art never expresses anything but itself." "Nothing that actually occurs is of the smallest importance." Form determines content, not content form, a point which Auden also sometimes affirms and which is often assumed by symbolists. With this theory Wilde turns Taine upon his head; the age does not determine what its art should be, rather it is art which gives the age its character. So far from responding to questions posed by the epoch, art offers answers before questions have been asked. "It is the ages that are her symbols." Life, straggling after art, seizes upon forms in art to express itself, so that life imitates art rather than art life. ". . . This unfortunate aphorism about Art holding the mirror up to Nature, is," according to Wilde, "deliberately said by Hamlet in order to convince the bystanders of his absolute insanity in all art-matters." If art be a mirror, we look into it to see—a mask. But more precisely, art is no mirror; it is a "mist of words," "a veil."

Sometimes the veil is pierced. This indifferent conferral of forms upon life by art may have unexpected consequences which implicate art instead of isolating it. In "The Decay of Lying" Wilde speaks of "silly boys who, after reading the adventures of Jack Sheppard or Dick Turpin, pillage the stalls of unfortunate applewomen, break into sweetshops at night, and alarm old gentlemen who are returning home from the city by leaping out on them in suburban lanes, with black masks and unloaded revolvers." In *Dorian Gray* the effect is more sinister; Dorian declares he has been poisoned by a book, and while Lord Henry assures him that art is too aloof to influence anybody, Dorian is felt to be right. Art may then transmit criminal impulses to his audience. Like Whitman, Wilde could and did say, "Nor will my poems do good only, they will do just as much evil, perhaps more."

The artist may be criminal and instill his work with criminality. Wilde's second essay in *Intentions* is "Pen Pencil and Poison." He uses Thomas Wainewright as the type of the artist. We need not expect to find a beautiful soul; Wainewright was instead "a forger of no mean or ordinary capabilities, and . . . a subtle and secret poisoner almost without rival in this or any age." Among his interesting tastes, Wainewright had "that curious love of green, which in individuals is always the sign of a subtle artistic temperament, and in nations is said to denote a laxity, if not a decadence of morals." When a friend reproached him with a murder, he shrugged his shoulders and gave an answer that Susan Sontag would call camp: "Yes; it was a dreadful thing to do, but she had very thick ankles." Wilde concludes that "the fact of a man being a poisoner is nothing against his prose," and "there is no essential incongruity between crime and culture." Wainewright's criminal career turns out to be strictly relevant to his art, fortifying it and giving it character. The quality of that art it is too early to judge, Wilde says, but he clearly believes that Wainewright's personality achieves sufficient criminality to have great artistic promise.

"The Critic as Artist" is the most ambitious of the essays in *Intentions*. It too conveys the notion that art undermines things as they are. The critic is the artist's accomplice in crime, or even masterminds the plot in which they are mutually engaged. Criticism overcomes the tendency of creation to repeat itself; it helps the artist discover unused possibilities. For at bottom, Wilde says, criticism is self-consciousness; it enables us to put our most recent phase at a distance and so go on to another. It disengages us so we may reengage ourselves in a new way.

From this argument Wilde proceeds to find criticism and self-consciousness to be as necessary as sin. "What is termed Sin is an essential element of progress"; without it, he holds, the world would stagnate or grow old or become colorless.

> By its curiosity [there is Arnold's word with Wilde's meaning] Sin increases the experience of the race. Through its intensified assertion of individualism it saves us from monotony of type. In its rejection of the current notions about morality, it is one with the highest ethics.

By a dexterous transvaluation of words, Wilde makes good and evil exchange places. Even socially sin is far more useful than martyrdom, he says, since it is self-expressive rather than self-repressive. The goal of man is the liberation of personality; when the day of true culture comes, sin will be impossible because the soul will be able to transform into elements of a richer experience, or a finer susceptibility, or a newer mode of thought, acts or passions that with the common would be commonplace, or with the uneducated ignoble, or with the shameful vile. Is this dangerous? Yes; it is dangerous—all ideas, as I told you, are so.

What muddies this point of view in Wilde is his looking back to conventional meanings of words like sin, ignoble, and shameful. He is not so ready as Nietzsche to transvaluate these, though he does reshuffle them. His private equation is that sin is the perception of new and dangerous possibilities in action as self-consciousness is in thought and criticism is in art. He espouses individualism, and he encourages society to make individualism more complete than it can be now, and for this reason he sponsors socialism as a communal egotism, like the society made up of separate but equal works of art.

Meantime, before socialism, what should be thought of the criminal impulses of the artist? Increasingly in his later writings, Wilde spreads the guilt from the artist to all men. If we are all insincere, masked, and lying, then the artist is prototype rather than exception. If all the sheep are black, then the artist cannot be blamed for not being white. Such an exculpation is implied in three of Wilde's plays after *Salome—Lady Windermere's Fan, A Woman of No Importance, An Ideal Husband.* Wilde allows his characters to be found guilty, but no guiltier than others, and more courageous in their wrongdoing.

Even as he defends them, he allows them to be mildly punished. Half-consciously, Wilde was preparing himself for another abrupt shift in his experience, such as he had made in 1886. It would be false to say that Wilde wanted to go to prison, yet the notion had frequently crossed his mind. He had always associated himself with the *poètes maudits,* always considered obloquy a certificate of literary merit. In "The Soul of Man under Socialism" he had opposed suffering, yet acknowledged that the Russian novelists had rediscovered a great medieval theme, the realization of man through suffering. More particularly, in a review of a new book of poems by Wilfrid Scawen Blunt in 1889, he began: "Prison has had an admirable effect on Mr. Wilfrid Blunt as a poet." It was like the effect of crime on Wainewright. Blunt had been merely witty and affected earlier, now his work had more depth. "Mr. Balfour must be praised," Wilde says jestingly, since "by sending Mr. Blunt to gaol . . . [he] has converted a clever rhymer into an earnest and deep-thinking poet." Six years later, just before his own disgrace, Wilde wrote in "The Soul of Man under Socialism," "After all, even in prison a man can be quite free." These hints indicate that Wilde was prepared, or thought he was, for trial and prison, and expected he would derive artistic profit from them. He had no idea of running away, even on a boyish holiday, whatever his friends might say. Instead he accepted imperial authority as readily as Christ had done—a precedent he discovered for himself, though hardly the first or last in hot water to do so. Blunt's poems written in prison were called *In Vinculis*, and Wilde's letter to Douglas from prison, which we know by Ross's title as *De Profundis*, was originally entitled by Wilde *Epistola: In Carcere et Vinculis*.

Hélas! Wilde's literary career was not transmogrified by prison as he hoped, but his experiences there, which were so much worse than he anticipated, gave him his final theme. *"La prison m'a complètement changé,"* he said to Gide at Berneval; *"je comptais sur elle pour cela."* As before, he made no effort to exonerate himself by saying that his sins were venial or not sins at all. Defenses of homosexual or "Uranian" love were common enough at this period; he did not make them. But he reached for the main implication of his disgrace through a double negative; though men thought he was unlike them, he was *not*. He was a genuine scapegoat.

This ultimate conception of himself was never put into an essay, but it is involved in his *De Profundis* letter to Douglas, and in *The Ballad of Reading Gaol*. Both are predictably full of imagery of Christ. Before this Wilde had depreciated pity as a motive in art; now he embraced it. The hero of his poem is a man who has murdered his mistress and is about to be hanged for his crime. Wilde identifies himself closely with this prisoner. The poem's tenor is that the prisoners are humanity, all of whom are felons:

> Yet each man kills the thing he loves,
> 　　By each let this be heard,
> Some do it with a bitter look,
> 　　Some with a flattering word,
> The coward does it with a kiss,
> 　　The brave man with a sword! . . .
>
> Some love too little, some too long,
> 　　Some sell, and others buy;
> Some do the deed with many tears,
> 　　And some without a sigh:
> For each man kills the thing he loves,
> 　　Yet each man does not die.

This poem was chosen for the *Oxford Book of Modern Verse* by Yeats, but he removed what he regarded as the commentary, including these stanzas. His effort to improve the poem evokes sympathy; it must be said, however, that whatever the quality of the bare narrative that Yeats prints, for Wilde—as for D. H. Lawrence and most readers—the commentary was the excessive and yet determining part of the poem. During the six years before his imprisonment he had demonstrated first that the artist was basically and usefully criminal, and second that criminality was not confined to artists, but was to be found as commonly among members of the Cabinet. Where most men pretend to a virtue they don't have, the artist, fully aware of his own sins, takes on those they don't acknowledge. The purpose of sin has subtly shifted in Wilde's mind—it is no longer a means for the artist of extending the boundaries of action, it is a means for him to focus and enshrine guilt. He has the courage, exceptional among men, of looking into the heart of things and finding there not brotherly love so much as murder, not self-love so much as suicide. In recognizing the universality of guilt he is like Christ; in revealing his own culpability he plays the role of his own Judas. Wilde, who had written in one of his poems that we are ourselves "the lips betraying and the life betrayed," had in fact brought about his own conviction. The result was that he was remarried to the society from which he had divorced himself; he was no outcast, for he accepted and even sought the punishment which other men, equally guilty, would only submit to vicariously through him, just as all the prisoners suffer with the doomed murderer. By means of submission and suffering he gives his life a new purpose, and writes over the palimpsest once again.

In this concern with social role Wilde has clearly moved away from Pater, and perhaps we can conceive of him as moving toward another writer, Jean Genet. Genet is of course ferocious and remorseless in a way that Wilde was not, and makes much less concession to the world. But the two men share an insistence on their own criminality and on a possible sanction for it. The comparison with Christ has been irresistible for both. As Genet says in *Thief's Journal:*

> Let us ignore the theologians. "Taking upon Himself the sins of the world" means exactly this: experiencing potentially and in their effects all sins; it means having subscribed to evil. Every creator must thus shoulder— the expression seems feeble—must make his own, to the point of knowing it to be his substance, circulating in his arteries, the evil given by him, which his heroes choose freely.

Wilde in *De Profundis* remembered having remarked to Gide that "there was nothing that . . . Christ had said that could not be transferred immediately into the sphere of Art, and there find its complete fulfilment." And again, Genet speaks like Wilde of the courage required to do wrong, saying: "If he has courage, the guilty man decides to be what crime has made him." He wishes to obtain "the recognition of evil." Both writers envisage a regeneration which can come only from total assumption of their proclivities and their lot; as Genet puts it:

> I shall destroy appearances, the casings will burn away and one evening I shall appear there, in the palm of your hand, quiet and pure, like a glass statuette. You will see me. Round about me there will be nothing left.

Wilde summons for this sacred moment a red rose growing from the hanged man's mouth, a white one from his heart. He had terrified André Gide by trying to persuade that strictly reared young man to authorize evil, as to some extent in the *acte gratuit* Gide did, and it is just such authorization that Genet asserts with more fierceness than Wilde.

In his criticism and in his work generally, Wilde balanced two ideas which, we have observed, look contradictory. One is that art is disengaged from actual life, the other that it is deeply incriminated with it. The first point of view is sometimes taken by Yeats, though only to qualify it, the second without qualification by Genet. That art is sterile, and that it is infectious, are attitudes not beyond reconciliation. Wilde never formulated their union, but he implied something like this: by its creation of beauty art reproaches the world, calling attention to the world's faults through their very omission; so the sterility of art is an affront or a parable. Art may also outrage the world by flouting its laws or by picturing indulgently their violation. Or art may seduce the world by making it follow an example which seems bad but is discovered to be better than it seems. In these various ways the artist forces the world toward self-recognition, with at least a tinge of self-redemption.

Yet this ethical or almost ethical view of art coexists in Wilde with its own cancelation. He could write *Salome* with one hand, dwelling upon incest and necrophilia, and show them as self-defeated, punished by execution and remorse. With the other hand, he could dissolve by the critical intellect all notions of sin and guilt. He does so in *The Importance of Being Earnest,* which is all insouciance where *Salome* is all incrimination. In *The Importance of Being Earnest* sins which are presented as accursed in *Salome* and unnameable in *Dorian Gray* are translated into a different key, and appear as Algernon's inordinate and selfish craving for—cucumber sandwiches. The substitution of mild gluttony for fearsome lechery renders all vice harmless. There *is* a wicked brother, but he is just our old friend Algernon. The double life which is so serious a matter for Dorian or for The Ideal Husband, becomes a harmless Bunburying, or playing Jack in the country and Ernest in town. In the earlier, four-act version of the play, Wilde even parodied punishment, by having a bailiff come to take Jack to Holloway Prison (as Wilde himself was soon to be taken) not for homosexuality, but for running up food bills at the Savoy. Jack is disinclined, he says, to be imprisoned in the suburbs for dining in town, and makes out a check. The notion of expiation is also mocked; as Cecily observes: "They have been eating muffins. That looks like repentance." Finally, the theme of regeneration is parodied in the efforts of Ernest and Jack to be baptized. (By the way, in the earlier version Prism is also about to be baptized, and someone comments, "To be born again would be of considerable advantage to her.") The ceremonial unmasking at the play's end, which had meant death for Dorian Gray, leaves everyone bare-faced for a new puppet show, that of matrimony. Yet amusing as it all is, much of the comedy derives from Wilde's own sense of the realities of what are being mocked. He was in only momentary refuge from his more usual cycle which ran from scapegrace to scapegoat.

During his stay in prison Wilde took up the regeneration theme in *De Profundis* and after being freed he resumed it in *The Ballad of Reading Gaol*. But he was too self-critical not to find the notion of rebirth a little preposterous. When his friends complained of his resuming old habits, he said, "A patriot put in prison for loving his country, loves his country, and a poet in prison for loving boys, loves boys." But to write about himself as unredeemed, unpunished, unreborn, to claim that his sins were nothing, that his form of love was more noble than most other people's, that what had happened to him was the result merely of legal obtuseness, was impossible for Wilde. So long as he had been a scapegrace the door to comedy was still open; once having accepted the role of scapegoat the door was closed. He conceived of a new play, but it was in his earlier mode and he could not write it. Cramped to one myth, and that somber and depleted, Wilde could not extricate himself. There was nothing to do but die, which accordingly he did. But not without one final assertion of a past enthusiasm: he was converted to Catholicism the night before his death.

CHRISTOPHER S. NASSAAR

The Darkening Lens

For a few seconds he stood bending over the balustrade, and peering down into the black seething well of darkness.

— The Picture of Dorian Gray

Ι t is doubtful that *The Picture of Dorian Gray* is "a great thing," but it has survived the test of time and is a deeper and more thoughtful novel than its critics have so far been willing to concede. The book is a strange one, a partly supernatural tale in which the characters are not individuals but symbols that move in a shadowy world of wit and terror. The novel is chiefly a study of various Victorian art movements corresponding to different stages in the development of Victorian human nature, and the main characters are meant to be person-ifications of these art movements and psychological states. Of central importance is the new art movement and type of person that was emerging in fin-de-siècle England. Dorian, as he degenerates, becomes a perfect example of the decadent, and his picture, as it grows more and more evil, a perfect type of decadent art.

The main difference between a morally committed aesthete and a decadent is that the latter, looking within and discovering not only purity but evil and corruption, yields to the corrupt impulse and tries to find joy and beauty in evil. Finally, the vision of evil becomes unbearable, the decadent has burned all his bridges, and he finds himself trapped in a dark underworld from which he cannot escape.

Lord Arthur Savile is an excellent example of the moral aesthete. Looking within, Arthur discovers not only the pure "Sybil" but also the corrupt and evil "Podgers." He rejects Podgers, however, and does everything in his power to marry Sybil. Finally, he is led by Providence to destroy Podgers and marry his love, thereby attaining a state of total purity.

The Picture of Dorian Gray is essentially a reversal of the situation in "Lord Arthur Savile's Crime." Sybil and Wotton represent the two opposing forces within Dorian, but Dorian, as soon as he becomes aware of the evil within himself, sells his soul in a fit of rebellion against the laws of God and nature. The determination of·*Dorian Gray*, moreover, contrasts with that of "Lord Arthur Savile's Crime." The idea of an external determining force is here abandoned in favor of a determinism whose springs well up from within the self:

> There are moments, psychologists tell us, when the passion for sin, or what the world calls sin, so dominates a nature, that every fibre of the body, as every cell of the brain, seems to be instinct with fearful impulses. Men and women at such moments lose the freedom of their will. They move to their terrible end as automatons move. Choice is taken from them, and conscience is either killed, or, if it lives at all, lives but to give rebellion its fascination, and disobedience its charm. For all sins, as theologians weary not of reminding us, are sins of disobedience. When that high spirit, that morning-star of evil, fell from heaven, it was as a rebel that he fell.
>
> Callous, concentrated on evil, with stained mind and soul hungry for rebellion, Dorian Gray hastened on, quickening his steps as he went.

A supernatural force does exist in the novel—it grants Dorian's demonic prayer—but that is its sole function. As it turns out, the devil Dorian sells his soul to is Lord Henry Wotton, who exists not only as something external to Dorian but also as a voice within him. *The Picture of Dorian Gray* is a psychological study of a nature—and an art movement—dominated by a passion for sin.

If we accept that Dorian died in 1890, the year in which *Dorian Gray* was mostly written and the earlier version published in *Lippincott's Magazine*, then the novel opens in the year 1873. We first meet Dorian shortly after he has passed the age of twenty, and he dies a few months after his thirty-eighth birthday, which he marks by murdering Basil. The novel thus traces Dorian's development over the span of approximately eighteen years, though Wilde's treatment of the passage of time in the novel is highly inadequate and is, perhaps, the book's most serious weak point.

The year 1873 was an important one for Oscar Wilde, for in that year Walter Pater published his *Studies in the History of the Renaissance.* Wilde is reported to have proclaimed during his first meeting with Yeats that *The Renaissance* "is my golden book; I never travel anywhere without it." Much later, in *De Profundis,* he broodingly referred to it as "that book which has had such a strange influence over my life." Indeed, *The Renaissance* casts a long, sinister shadow across *The Picture of Dorian Gray,* and the entire novel seems to be structured with Pater's book as its focal point.

The Picture of Dorian Gray begins in Basil Hallward's studio, with a conversation between Basil and Lord Henry Wotton. These are the two artists in the novel, Basil's art being his painting while Wotton's is his conversation. The two men are opposites: Basil is a largely pure man who yields to a streak of evil in his soul, while Wotton is a highly corrupt man who never commits an immoral action. Basil's attachment to Dorian has a homosexual dimension, and his disappearances are probably for the sake of homosexual relief. (This is clear in the earlier, shorter version of the novel, but Wilde toned it down considerably in the later version.) As for Wotton, Basil says to him: "You are an extraordinary fellow. You never say a moral thing, and you never do a wrong thing." Basil's purity is balanced against Wotton's corruption, while Basil's wrong actions stand opposite to Wotton's entirely moral existence.

Basil paints Dorian while Dorian is still in a state of innocence. "He seems to me little more than a lad, though he is really over twenty," Basil says; and Wotton, when he first sets eyes on Dorian, corroborates this view: "Lord Henry looked at him. . . . There was something in his face that made him trust him at once. All the candour of youth was there, as well as all youth's passionate purity. One felt that he had kept himself unspotted from the world." The painting is Basil's masterpiece because Dorian is the flawless manifestation of Basil's lost innocence. It is not until Dorian begins to respond to Wotton's poisonous sermon, however, that the picture becomes complete, for the faint flush of evil that comes across Dorian's face renders him the perfect embodiment of the painter's soul, and allows Basil to introduce the finishing touch to his masterpiece.

As I have said, the chief characters in *The Picture of Dorian Gray* are both human types and representatives of different art movements. This is clearest in Dorian, who exists both as a picture and as a human. This neat split allows us to separate decadence as an art movement from decadence as a mode of life, and to examine the two separately. Wilde clouds the issue, however, by making Wotton fasten on the live Dorian and, paradoxically, treat the breathing human being as a work of art. Basil expounds a theory of art straight out of Pater's essay on Leonardo in *The Renaissance.* The artist, Basil argues, searches in the outside world for the perfect manifestation of his own soul. When he finds this object, he can create masterpieces by painting it. Moreover, the proximity of this object can inspire the artist to trace his own soul in the forms of nature. Wotton muses on this theory, then reverses it by deciding to recreate Dorian the human until he becomes a perfect external manifestation of Wotton's own soul:

> He was a marvellous type, too, this lad, whom by so curious a chance he had met in Basil's studio, or could be fashioned into a marvellous type, at any rate. Grace was his, and the white purity of boyhood, and beauty such as old Greek marbles kept for us. There was nothing one could not do with him. He could be made a Titan or a toy.
> Yes, he would try to be to Dorian Gray what, without knowing it, the lad had been to the painter who had fashioned the wonderful portrait. He would seek to dominate him—had already, indeed, done so. He would make that wonderful spirit his own.

That Wotton regards Dorian as an instrument for his art is clear from the way he thinks about him. In the above quotation, he seems to regard himself as a sculptor and Dorian's placid Greek soul as his clay. Here is another example of Wotton's thinking about Dorian: "Talking to him was like playing upon an exquisite violin. He answered to every touch and thrill of the bow."

The process of recreating Dorian begins in Basil's studio, when Wotton preaches an invidious sermon based heavily on the Conclusion of Pater's *Renaissance.* There is an important difference between Pater and Wotton, however. Wotton, by substituting the word *sensations* for the word *impressions,* slightly but significantly modifies Pater's doctrine. Pater had written: "With this sense of the splendour of our experience and of its awful brevity, gathering all we are into one desperate effort to see and touch, we shall hardly have time to make theories about the things we see and touch. What we have to do is to be for ever curiously testing new opinions and courting new impressions." Wotton, on the other hand, preaches to Dorian: "Live! Live the wonderful life that is in you! Let nothing be lost upon you. Be always searching for new sensations."

The Conclusion to Pater's *Renaissance* was widely misinterpreted by the young men of his day, who understood it as a call to live a life of indiscriminate sensations—a fact that led Pater to suppress the Conclusion in the second edition of his book. Wilde was too intelligent to have misunderstood Pater's concluding chapter, but it was precisely this Conclusion that sparked the decadent movement in England. And since *The Picture of Dorian Gray* is primarily an examination of the decadent movement, it is proper that Wotton should present Pater's doctrine as it was understood by the decadents, not as Pater meant it to be understood.

There is more to the matter than that, however. In the third edition of *The Renaissance* (1888), Pater restored his Conclusion, but made "some slight changes which bring it closer to my original meaning." The changes are really insignificant, but it is possible, even probable, that Wilde also believed Pater's original meaning needed to be clearly brought out through some "slight changes." The modifications Wotton makes in Pater's Conclusion can therefore be seen as bringing it closer to what Wilde felt was Pater's original meaning. Wotton would then suggest—as Richard Ellmann believes—Walter Pater himself, but Pater as Wilde understood him. "In *The Picture of Dorian Gray*," Ellmann tells us, "Pater is enclosed (like an unhappy dryad caught in a tree trunk) in Lord Henry Wotton. Lord Henry's chief sin is quoting without acknowledgment from *The Renaissance*. . . . Pater, who wrote a review of [*Dorian Gray*], was at great pains to distinguish Lord Henry's philosophy from his own. Wilde seems to have intended not to distinguish them, however, and to offer (through the disastrous effects of Lord Henry's influence upon Dorian) a criticism of Pater."

Wotton's demonic sermon destroys Dorian's state of innocence and plunges him into a state of experience. Paradoxically, Basil has already paved the way for Wotton by excessively worshipping Dorian's physical beauty and making Dorian aware of this beauty. The sermon begs the evil in Dorian to blossom forth, and he responds splendidly:

> He was dimly conscious that entirely fresh influences were at work within him. Yet they seemed to have come really from himself. The few words that Basil's friend had said to him—words spoken by chance, no doubt, and with wilful paradox in them—had touched some secret chord that had never been touched before, but that he felt was now vibrating and throbbing to curious pulses.
>
> Music had stirred him like that. Music had troubled him many times. But music was not articulate. It was not a new world, but rather another chaos, that it created in us. Mere words! How terrible they were! How clear, and vivid, and cruel! One could not escape from them. And yet what a subtle magic there was in them! They seemed to be able to give a plastic form to formless things, and to have a music of their own as sweet as that of viol or of lute.

Wotton's words are associated with music, which is an art. Basil is an artist who uses a brush, but Wotton is an artist who uses words. He is the decadent artist, who will recreate his evil soul in Dorian and derive pleasure from contemplating his demonic creation.

Wotton's words, however, seem to Dorian to come from within himself, for Wotton as artist is the external manifestation of the evil in Dorian. In Oscar Wilde's works, the movement of negative capability is often reversed, so that the main character seems to absorb the others into himself. Dorian, under the influence of Wotton's sermon, immediately sells his soul to the devil. Symbolically, what this means is that Dorian cannot and never will be able to resist the evil within himself—that is, the voice of Wotton. His passion for sin will be the governing principle of his life.

In his new thirst for sensations, Dorian's first action is to fall in love with Sybil Vane. The development of the decadent is a gradual process, and Dorian, newly emerged from a state of innocence, at first seeks pure sensations remote from evil. It is clear, though, that his love for Sybil Vane—in contrast to Lord Arthur's love for his Sybil—is Dorian's first decadent act. He says to Wotton:

> It would never have happened if I had not met you. You filled me with a wild desire to know everything about life. For days after I met you, something seemed to throb in my veins. As I lounged in the Park, or strolled down Piccadilly, I used to look at everyone who passed me, and wonder, with a mad curiosity, what sort of lives they led. Some of them fascinated me. Others filled me with terror. There was an exquisite poison in the air. I had a passion for sensations.

Dorian spiritualizes his attachment to Sybil and deceives himself about its highly sensual nature, but Wotton is very aware that the attachment is Dorian's first step in his development as a decadent. This is Wotton's reaction as Dorian raves about Sybil's purity and divinity:

> Lord Henry watched him with a subtle sense of pleasure. How different he was now from the shy, frightened boy he had met in Basil Hallward's studio! His nature had blossomed like a flower, had borne blossoms of scarlet flame. Out of its secret hiding-place had crept his Soul, and Desire had come to meet it on the way.

Sybil is a character who knows nothing of evil. Unlike her counterpart in "Lord Arthur Savile's Crime," however, she exists in a childlike world of innocence, and it is stressed over and over again that she is still immature. "There is something of a child about her," says Dorian, and goes on to say that when they first met they "stood looking at each other like children." Sybil, moreover, is presented not as an individual but as the embodiment of a state of the soul and an entire movement in Victorian art. Pater, in *The Renaissance*, wrote of the Mona Lisa that she is the symbol of modern human nature, "of what in the ways of a thousand years men had come to desire":

> Hers is the head upon which all "the ends of the world are come," and the eyelids are a little weary. It is a beauty wrought out from within upon the flesh, the deposit, little cell by cell, of strange thoughts and fantastic reveries and exquisite passions. Set it for a moment beside one of those white Greek goddesses or beautiful women of antiquity, and how would they be troubled by this beauty, into which the soul with all its maladies has passed! . . .
>
> The fancy of a perpetual life, sweeping together ten thousand experiences, is an old one; and modern thought has conceived the idea of humanity as wrought upon by, and summing up in itself, all modes of thought and life. Certainly Lady Lisa might stand as the embodiment of the old fancy, the symbol of the modern idea.

If the Mona Lisa is Pater's symbol of the modern idea, Sybil is Wilde's symbol of the old idea, gathering together ten thousand experiences and embodying in herself the world's purity. Dorian says of her: "I have seen her in every age and in every costume. Ordinary women never appeal to one's imagination. They are limited to their century." And again: "She is all the great heroines of the world in one. She is more than an individual." Pater had written of Greek art that it is too serene and undisturbed to satisfy us, for in ancient Greece the human race was still in its infancy, unaware of the seriousness and terror of evil and still uninfected by any spiritual sickness. Modern art, he held, must deal with the grotesque—with life, conflict, evil—for the evolution of the human spirit has made us terribly aware of the dark, evil caverns in human nature, and it is from this new situation that art must now try to wrest joy. The white Greek goddesses and beautiful women of antiquity no longer satisfy us.

Sybil, serene and untouched by any knowledge of evil, represents the Hellenic ideal. She has a "Greek head," and her name connects her with Greek mythology. When she appears in a play, it is invariably in the role of the spotless heroine—Juliet or Imogen or Rosalind—and Basil and Dorian see her purpose as that of spiritualizing the age. She is the visible symbol of an art and a state of the soul whose beauty is one of purity peculiar to the infancy of the race or of an age. Sybil exists in naturalistic surroundings—she acts in "an absurd little theatre, with great flaring gas-jets and gaudy play-bills," presided over by a "hideous Jew" who smokes "a vile cigar"—but her artistic imagination transforms her corrupt environment and renders it pure and spotless. Her imagination also transforms Dorian, for she sees him as entirely pure and untouched by evil at a time when he is already under Wotton's influence. For Sybil, Dorian is a fairy-tale prince out of the pages of literature:

> "She said quite simply to me, 'You look like a prince. I must call you Prince Charming.'"
>
> "Upon my word, Dorian, Miss Sybil knows how to pay compliments."
>
> "You don't understand her, Harry. She regarded me merely as a person in a play. She knows nothing of life."

Sybil, however, is a child who cannot come of age and survive. She exists in a protective world of art from which she cannot emerge without dying. Her projected marriage to Dorian coaxes her out of this world and causes her to come into contact with the demon universe. Pater, in the Conclusion to *The Renaissance,* maintained that success in life is to achieve a state of constant ecstasy, to burn always with a hard, gemlike flame, and ended his chapter thus:

> Great passions may give us this quickened sense of life, ecstasy and sorrow of love, the various forms of enthusiastic activity, disinterested or otherwise, which come naturally to many of us. Only be sure it is passion—that it does yield you this fruit of a quickened, multiplied consciousness. Of this wisdom, the poetic passion, the desire of beauty, the love of art for art's sake, has most; for art comes to you professing frankly to give nothing but the highest quality to your moments as they pass, and simply for those moments' sake.

It is art, then, that can give the highest quality to our moments, that can fire us with a constant flamelike ecstasy. Paradoxically, Sybil—in order to achieve this flamelike ecstasy—rejects art for life, for a great passion. After she gives her terrible performance in front of Basil and Wotton, Dorian rushes backstage to find that "the girl was standing there alone, with a look of triumph on her face. Her eyes were lit with an exquisite fire. There was a radiance about her. Her parted lips were smiling over some secret of their own." She says to him: "You have made me understand what love really is. My love! my love! Prince Charming! Prince of life! I have grown sick of shadows. You are more to me than all art can ever be." Prince Charming is no longer a character out of a play but is now the prince of life.

When Sybil's world of art is shattered, her imagination ceases to recreate the outside world and render it pure and spotless. As a consequence, she becomes aware of the sordid side of life:

> To-night, for the first time in my life, I saw through the hollowness, the sham, the silliness of the empty pageant in which I had always played. To-night, for the first time, I became conscious that the Romeo was hideous, and old, and painted, that the moonlight in the orchard was false, that the scenery was vulgar, and that the words I had to speak were unreal, were not my words, were not what I wanted to say.

Sybil, however, is too fragile to confront the demonic and survive. The death blow falls when she becomes aware of the evil in Dorian. Dorian had loved her as an erotic symbol of purity, but when she rejects art for life, she loses her ability to isolate herself from "the stain of an age . . . at once sordid and sensual." Like the protagonists of the fairy tales, she moves from innocence into experience, but as soon as she enters the demonic world of the naturalists, she begins to have naturalistic experiences. Dorian callously walks out on her, and she dies by swallowing "some dreadful thing they use at theatres," with white lead or prussic acid in it. Her lonely suicide in a tawdry actress's dressing room is straight Zola. This is how people die in naturalist literature—not on the high seas or in Horatio's arms, but alone, in poverty and despair. Wotton reflects on her death, "The moment she touched actual life she marred it, and it marred her, and so she passed away."

Sybil's death has dimensions that far transcend her death as the result of a psychological state. "Without your art you are nothing," Dorian informs her, and indeed her death symbolizes the death of an entire movement in art. Sybil is inseparable from art. Dorian says:

> On the first night I was at the theatre, the horrid old Jew came round to the box after the performance was over, and offered to take me behind the scenes and introduce me to her. I was furious with him, and told him that Juliet had been dead for hundreds of years, and that her body was lying in a marble tomb in Verona. I think, from his blank look of amazement, that he was under the impression that I had taken too much champagne, or something.

Pater saw the Mona Lisa as the supreme example of modern art, for modern art must encompass all of human nature, in all its evil and terror, and present it in a way that makes it beautiful. He saw the portrait of *La Gioconda* as combining in its chill beauty the pure and evil strains in human nature—as summing up human nature from a modern perspective. Humanity, for Pater, has developed beyond its initial state of innocence and can no longer be satisfied with an art that cannot deal with evil. Wilde, in *Dorian Gray*, modifies Pater's idea and applies it to the Victorian world as a separate entity, as though the human race had been born anew at the beginning of the Victorian period. Ian Fletcher has observed that

"Pater's method, in *The Renaissance*," is to explore "not so much a period as a movement of history through selected individuals." Wilde's method is the same, but he focuses instead on the movement of a single period, presenting the Victorians as having begun in placid innocence but developed beyond it.

Sybil is the symbol of the innocence of the Victorians, both in life and in art. She represents a movement in art that knows nothing of evil and dwells in a beautiful, private world. In this respect, she suggests Tennyson more than anyone else. The early Tennyson wrote poetry that was serenely unaware of evil and that advocated an isolated existence in a dazzling, beautiful world of art. It is precisely such a world that the poet seeks and finds in "Recollections of the Arabian Nights." The ivory tower of serene artistic delight is very much the message of Tennyson's early poetry. "The Palace of Art" and "The Lady of Shalott," however, reflect his growing dissatisfaction with this private world. And in *In Memoriam*, the beautiful art world crumbles and Tennyson confronts the demonic, mid-Victorian scientific universe.

Like Sybil, moreover, Tennyson tumbles from his ivory tower into the demon universe because of a great love. Unlike Sybil, though, he paradoxically survives to retreat into the world of Arthurian romance and to write about a virtuous king who is finally destroyed by evil forces outside himself. Interestingly, "The Last Tournament," one of the grimmest and darkest of the Idylls, was published in 1872, and Tennyson at the time meant it as the continuation and conclusion of *The Idylls of the King* ("The Passing of Arthur" had appeared earlier, in 1869). In 1885, he published another Idyll, "Balin and Balan," but that was to appear toward the middle of the sequence, not—like "The Passing of Arthur" and "The Last Tournament"—at the end. *The Idylls of the King* may be said to be Tennyson's last great work. Much of his time after 1872 was devoted to an unsuccessful attempt to storm the English stage with a series of historical tragedies, until in 1884 he gave up in despair.

It is probably the art movement of Tennyson that Sybil is meant to represent. He looked to past ages and foreign lands in his poetry, and Sybil always appears in plays belonging to past centuries and set in foreign lands. Her relationship with Dorian, moreover, clearly suggests the Lady of Shalott, and she indeed echoes her when she rejects art and says to her lover, "I have grown sick of shadows." The art of an age can isolate itself from evil only during the infancy of that age. As the age matures, such art movements must collapse as evil presses in on them. Consequently Sybil, the symbol of an innocent movement in Victorian art, dies. The Satanic

Wotton reflects: "There is something to me quite beautiful about her death. I am glad I am living in a century when such wonders happen."

Sybil's mother and brother, like Sybil, represent a trend in art that belongs to the innocence of the Victorians, and they too are inseparable from the movement they symbolize. Wilde tells us of Jim Vane: "He was thick-set of figure, and his hands and feet were large, and somewhat clumsy in movement. He was not so finely bred as his sister. One would hardly have guessed the close relationship that existed between them." And yet a very close relationship does exist. Whereas Sybil represented the innocence of the Victorians at a very high artistic level, Jim represents the same thing at a much lower level. James Vane and his mother are straight out of Victorian melodrama, and Victorian melodrama, in its infantile treatment of evil, its lack of intellectual content, its presentation of heroes who always triumph and black villains who are always defeated, is a drama of childlike innocence. Jim Vane is not an individual but a type. To Sybil's artistic imagination, he is all the heroes of Victorian melodrama rolled into one. His future is envisioned by his sister:

> He was to leave the vessel at Melbourne, bid a polite good-bye to the captain, and go off at once to the gold-fields. Before a week was over he was to come across a large nugget of pure gold, the largest nugget that had ever been discovered, and bring it down to the coast in a waggon guarded by six mounted policemen. The bush-rangers were to attack them three times, and be defeated with immense slaughter. Or, no. He was not to go to the gold-fields at all. They were horrid places, where men got intoxicated, and shot each other in bar-rooms, and used bad language. He was to be a nice sheep-farmer, and one evening, as he was riding home, he was to see the beautiful heiress being carried off by a robber on a black horse, and give chase, and rescue her. Of course she would fall in love with him, and he with her, and they would get married, and come home, and live in an immense house in London. Yes, there were delightful things in store for him.

The specific events in Jim's future are uncertain, but what is certain is that there are delightful, melodramatic things in store for him. And indeed, if he were acting in a melodrama there would be no question about that. Jim's tragedy, however, is similar to his sister's: he rejects art for life. Instead of joining the group, as his mother had wished, he decides to become a real-life sailor and says to his mother: "I should like to make some money to take you and Sybil off the stage. I hate it." By rejecting the stage, however, he becomes part of the terrible world of the naturalists. He continues to behave melodramatically in this world, making wild threats against Sybil's aristocratic lover, and Sybil says to him: "Oh, don't be so serious, Jim. You are like one of the heroes of those silly melodramas mother used to be so fond of acting in." When we meet Jim again, nearly eighteen years later, he is associated with loathsome dens, dark alleys, old hags, and the filth of port life. This is the world of the naturalists, but he continues to behave melodramatically in it. He is mistakenly shot and killed while hiding behind a bush—an unthinkable end for a stout-hearted British sailor in a proper melodrama, but a very usual end for a character in naturalist literature.

Sybil's mother is a secondary character, but she is a counterpoint to her son in that she is a melodramatic figure who clings on to the stage. She yearns for the days when melodrama was popular, and she compensates by trying to mold her life into a melodrama. This is how she reacts to Sybil:

> "Ah! mother, mother, let me be happy!"
> Mrs. Vane glanced at her, and with one of those false theatrical gestures that so often becomes a mode of second nature to a stage-player, clasped her in her arms.

And again:

> "Kiss me, mother," said the girl. Her flower-like lips touched the withered cheek, and warmed its frost.
> "My child! my child!" cried Mrs. Vane, looking up to the ceiling in search of an imaginary gallery.

Mrs. Vane absolutely must exist in a melodramatic atmosphere. She has outlived her time, however, and she suggests more than anything else a defeated character in a naturalistic novel. The "silly melodramas" she "used to be so fond of acting in" were probably of the *Black-Eyed Susan* and *Luke the Labourer* variety. As early as the 1860s, these crude melodramas were already on the decline. "By the 1860's melodramas were simply better written than they had been earlier. Characters remained types, but touches of subtlety and complexity appeared in characterization. Slapstick was replaced by witty repartee. Restrained sentiment now and then replaced tear-jerking sentimentality." The sordid world of the naturalists, moreover, infiltrated the melodrama in the 1860s and began to make appearances in the plays of Boucicault—in his famous melodrama, *After Dark,* for instance. By the 1890s, the old-fashioned branch of the melodrama had died out. The new and more vigorous branch had evolved into the new drama. Mrs. Vane dies after her daughter but before her son. Indeed, Wilde presents her as in a sense already dead, for she is old and withered and decayed. The Victorians having emerged from their state of innocence, melodrama is inevitably in a state of decay, moving toward certain death.

Sybil's rejection of art and her subsequent suicide constitute a further deliverance of Dorian into the hands of the devil. Dorian says to Wotton at one point, concerning Sybil:

> And her voice—I never heard such a voice. It was very low at first, with deep mellow notes, that seemed to fall singly upon one's ear. Then it became a little louder, and sounded like a flute or a distant hautbois. In the garden-scene it had all the tremulous ecstasy that one hears just before dawn when nightingales are singing. There were moments, later on, when it had the wild passion of violins. You know how a voice can stir one. Your voice and the voice of Sybil Vane are two things I shall never forget. When I close my eyes, I hear them, and each of them says something different. I don't know which to follow.

The passage recalls an earlier one, already quoted, giving Dorian's reaction to Wotton's voice. Dorian's nature is gray: good and evil are locked in mortal combat within him. Wotton is the voice of evil, while Sybil, reinforced by Basil, is the voice of goodness. When Sybil dies, Basil becomes exclusively the voice of goodness for Dorian, but the voice comes primarily from within Dorian, and the murder of Basil, instead of silencing it, only intensifies it. It is Dorian's destiny, however, to yield to the evil voice within himself. He has, after all, sold his soul to the devil:

> "I wish now I had not told you about Sybil Vane."
> "You could not have helped telling me, Dorian. All through your life you will tell me everything you do."
> "Yes, Harry, I believe that is true. I cannot help telling you things. You have a curious influence over me."

At one point, Lord Henry Wotton says to Dorian: "A new Hedonism— that is what our century wants. You might be its visible symbol." It is Dorian's destiny to be the perfect embodiment of this new hedonism—of decadence.

Before Sybil's death, Dorian searches for pure sensations. After her death, the sensations he seeks become less and less pure. He falls heavily under the spell of a mysterious yellow book—usually identified as Huysmans's À Rebours—and this is a crucial stage in his development as a decadent, although it is only chapter 11 and the final pages of chapter 10 that record the yellow book's evil influence. Since the yellow book forms such an important stage in Dorian's development, it is necessary to understand what Wilde meant it to suggest. Wilde wrote, in chapter 11, that one has "ancestors in literature, as well as in one's own race, nearer perhaps in type and temperament, many of them, and certainly with an influence of which one was more absolutely conscious."

The two major influences on the English decadent movement were Pater's *The Renaissance* (1873) and Joris-Karl Huysmans's *À Rebours* (1884). The yellow book is a nonexistent combination of these two works, one English and the other French; Dorian, it will be recalled, was born of an English father and a French mother. Although chapter 11 mostly reflects *À Rebours*, strong echoes of *The Renaissance* also occur, mostly toward the beginning. Dorian remains under the spell of the yellow book for eighteen years, moreover, and if we accept that he died in 1890—the year in which most of *The Picture of Dorian Gray* was written and the earlier version published—then it becomes impossible to see the yellow book as being simply *À Rebours* and very easy to recognize it as also being partly *The Renaissance*.

Through the yellow book and because of it, the post-Sybil Dorian experiences the history of the entire human race, precisely as Huysmans's hero did, and learns everything that Pater asserted modern man already knows: "It seemed to him that in exquisite raiment, and to the delicate sound of flutes, the sins of the world were passing in dumb show before him. Things that he had dimly dreamed of were suddenly made real to him. Things of which he had never dreamed were gradually revealed." Finally, Dorian comes to feel that he has absorbed everything the human race has ever known, especially its evil passions and sensations: "There were times when it seemed to Dorian Gray that the whole of history was merely the record of his own life, not as he had lived it in act and circumstance, but as his imagination had created it for him, as it had been in his brain and in his passions. He felt that he had known them all, those strange terrible figures that had passed across the stage of the world and made sin so marvellous and evil so full of subtlety. It seemed to him that in some mysterious way their lives had been his own."

Dorian, however, will go beyond anything the race—including Des Esseintes and the modern Paterian man—has yet known, and will become the visible symbol of Wotton's new hedonism. The yellow book teaches him an important lesson. Wilde ends chapter 11 thus: "Dorian Gray had been poisoned by a book. There were moments when he looked on evil simply as a mode through which he could realise his conception of the beautiful." The book teaches Dorian to seek beauty in evil, and as he comes to depend more and more on evil and evil sensations in his search for beauty, he becomes a full-blown decadent. Along with the detailed record in chapter 11 of Dorian's interest in jewels and perfumes, lengthy and mysterious absences are mentioned, after which he creeps back home, goes to the locked room and gazes with joy at his grinning, sin-scarred portrait, the mirror of his soul, gleefully comparing it with the beautiful mask that is his body: "He grew more and more enamoured of his own beauty, *more and more interested in the corruption of his own soul.* He would examine with minute care, and sometimes with a monstrous and terrible delight, the hideous lines that seared the wrinkling forehead or crawled around the heavy sensual mouth, wondering sometimes which were the more horrible, the signs of sin or the signs of age" (italics mine). The portrait is in the process of becoming a decadent work of art. The hideous, evil portrait, and Dorian's gleeful reaction to it, typifies a very important aspect of that art—the delighted recognition and celebration of the evil within the soul. We later learn—just before Basil's murder—that the portrait has "grinning lips." Decadent art, like aesthetic art, deals to a large extent with the world within, but while moral aesthetic art—Rossetti's is the major example—presents the soul as being essentially pure, decadent art sees it as being evil and derives pleasure from this evil.

The decadent poetry of Arthur Symons, for instance, is largely a sensually rendered exploration—often a celebration—of the poet's "spiritual and moral perversity." Enid Starkie, in *From Gautier to Eliot,* has noted the influence of the French symbolist movement on Symons's decadent poetry. In "The Decadent Movement in Literature" (1893), Symons did not much differentiate between the terms *decadent* and *symbolist,* and he described decadence as a "beautiful and interesting disease." More recently, James Nelson, in *The Early Nineties: A View From the Bodley Head,* has examined the poems of *Silhouettes* (1892) and found them in the French impressionist and symbolist vein, the chief influence being Verlaine. Nelson tells us that "Symons was fascinated by the whirling sights, the silhouettes dark against the light of the gas jets, the smoke, the talk, and the music of the café-dance hall and found in such haunts men like puppets abandoning themselves to a kind of madness and oblivion born of disillusionment and despair. But perhaps of even more interest to him was the kind of beauty found there, a tainted beauty all the more fascinating and significant for its signs of evil and artifice." In "Javanese Dancers," which Nelson rightly calls "a symbolist poem," he finds "Symons' most potent evocation of an evil beauty comparable to something perhaps only Beardsley could create." The poem's central dancer, who radiates a strange, bewitchingly demonic beauty, appears on the stage

> Smiling between her painted lids a smile
> Motionless, unintelligible, she twines
> Her fingers into mazy lines,
> Twining her scarves across them all the while.

As Nelson observes, this central dancer is "essentially what Frank Kermode has described as the Romantic Image." Her sensuous, undulating form is a symbol of perfect harmony, fusing together the opposites of body and soul, of the outer world Symons is contemplating and the world within himself. Her body, which Symons worships, is also that fascinating disease, his own corrupt soul.

If the poems of *Silhouettes* are largely dominated by a gray mood of pessimism, those of *London Nights* (1895) are unified by a heated, hungry sensuality. These poems must not be read simply as a celebration of lust, however. The voluptuous harlots and abandoned women who fill the pages of *London Nights* are heavily sensuous, erotic symbols in the outer world of Symons's tainted, evil soul. In the opening poem of the volume, "Prologue," Symons indicates to us how the poems of *London Nights* should be approached. The tone of "Prologue" is one of dismay rather than delight, but the symbols are clearly identified as such:

> My life is like a music-hall,
> Where, in the impotence of rage,
> Chained by enchantment to my stall,
> I see myself upon the stage
> Dance to amuse a music-hall.
>
> 'Tis I that smoke this cigarette,
> Lounge here, and laugh for vacancy,
> And watch the dancers turn; and yet
> It is my very self I see
> Across the cloudy cigarette.
>
> My very self that turns and trips,
> Painted, pathetically gay,
> An empty song upon the lips
> In make-believe of holiday:
> I, I, this thing that turns and trips!
>
> The light flares in the music-hall,
> The light, the sound, that weary us;
> Hour follows hour, I count them all,
> Lagging, and loud, and riotous:
> My life is like a music-hall.

In the brief but important preface to the second edition of *London Nights*, Symons suggests that "the whole visible world . . . is but a symbol, made visible in order that we may apprehend ourselves, and not be blown hither and thither like a flame in the night." Symons recognized the painted dancers he sought in music halls and the harlots he embraced as being symbols in the visible world of the soul within himself, and the poems of *London Nights*—for all their heated sensuality—attempt to go beneath the surface of things to explore and celebrate the perverse, evil world within. In "Stella Maris," for instance (which first appeared separately in *The Yellow Book* in 1894), Symons celebrates a night of delirious lust as "that ineffable delight / When souls turn bodies, and unite / In the intolerable, the whole / Rapture of the embodied soul." In "Liber Amoris," he informs us that once, long ago, "I loved good women," but adds ironically that, "for a body and soul like mine, / I found the angels' food too fine."

The soul seeks that in the visible world which most approximates its own nature, and instead of worshiping blessed damozels like Rossetti, Symons yields passionately to lust and vice, adoring, rather, the seductive Bianca, whose "illusive change, / The strangeness of your smile, the faint/ Corruption of your gaze," is reminiscent of the Mona Lisa as described in Pater's *Renaissance*. He ends his poem with the daring line, "So Bianca satisfies my soul." Like Dorian, Symons seems to have "had mad hungers that grew more ravenous as he fed them," but also like Dorian, he was at this point very deeply "interested in the corruption of his own soul."

Similarly, John Gray, in the poems that make up his volume of decadent verse, *Silverpoints* (1893), has for one of his main themes the identification and celebration of the evil within the human soul. Here is one of the best of his poems, titled simply "Poem":

> Geranium, houseleek, laid in oblong beds
> On the trim grass. The daisies' leprous stain
> Is fresh. Each night the daisies burst again,
> Though every day the gardener crops their heads.
>
> A wistful child, in foul unwholesome shreds,
> Recalls some legend of a daisy chain
> That makes a pretty necklace. She would fain
> Make one, and wear it, if she had some threads.
>
> Sun, leprous flowers, foul child. The asphalt burns.
> The garrulous sparrows perch on metal Burns.
> Sing! Sing! they say, and flutter with their wings.
> He does not sing, he only wonders why
> He is sitting there. The sparrows sing. And I
> Yield to the strait allure of simple things.

In the first stanza, nature is represented as evil. The gardener attempts to suppress and control the evil daisies, but every night they burst again and their leprous stain remains fresh. In the second stanza, a child recalls some vague, romantic legend about daisies—Wordsworth's "To the Daisy" poems come to mind here—but the child, ironically, is foul and yearns to make "a pretty necklace" of the leprous flowers, and wear it around her neck. In the third stanza, the life-giving sun, leprous flowers, and foul child unite to form an unholy trinity. The sun is scorching and it makes the asphalt—a symbol of civilization—burn with its oppressive heat. The metal statue of Burns is totally out of place in this un-Romantic setting, but the garrulous sparrows, symbols of uncontrolled nature, are quite at home, and they sing as they perch on the silent statue of the Romantic poet.

This garden setting is entirely in accord with the evil nature of John Gray, and he ends his poem by yielding happily "to the strait allure of simple things." In "Poem," Gray celebrates evil, locates it both within himself and in the outside world, and embraces it. Almost a century before, Wordsworth had "heard a thousand blended notes, / While in a grove I sate reclined," and had said that "To her fair works did Nature link / The human soul that through me ran." Gray's human soul links with a nature that is the antithesis of Wordsworth's—a nature thrilling with evil beauty.

Dorian's grinning, evil portrait, then, and his delighted reaction to it, is typical of one very important aspect of decadent art—the gleeful recognition and celebration of a depravity whose wellsprings are within the soul.

The Pre-Raphaelite movement in England, dominated by the figure of Dante Gabriel Rossetti, began toward the middle of the nineteenth century and was on the wane by 1890. In *The Picture of Dorian Gray*, Basil Hallward is the representative of this movement. In his very photographic approach to painting, Basil suggests Holman Hunt, and perhaps also John Everett Millais, both members of the original Pre-Raphaelite Brotherhood. Jerome Buckley has observed of Hunt that "to perceive intensely and to paint with absolute 'truth to nature' were the first principles of his Pre-Raphaelite creed." In his paintings, Hunt strove for absolute authenticity in every last detail. For instance, "The Scapegoat" was "modelled by a real goat tethered in woebegone thirst by the actual shore of the Dead Sea." The background of "The Triumph of the Innocents," moreover, was "drawn with photographic fidelity on the very road from Jerusalem to Bethlehem."

Basil, however, largely suggests Rossetti. Buckley has written of Rossetti: "Both as painter and as poet, Rossetti, though attentive always to detail, was more literary than literal, interested first of all in the psychology of moods, the analysis of states of soul, and eager to depict the life of an imagination nourished on books and private reverie." Far more anxiously than his disciples, however, "Rossetti sought to make the sharp sense impression the avenue to mystical revelation." In his paintings and writings, Rossetti presented women chiefly as sensuous manifestations of total spiritual purity—a purity he deeply yearned for and found personified in Elizabeth Siddal and Jane Morris. In Rossetti's early short story, "Hand and Soul," the beautiful, ethereal lady who appears in Chiaro's room and bids him serve God by painting her, identifies herself as his soul. There was a demonic streak in Rossetti's soul, however, and this is vividly expressed, for instance, in his portrait of Lilith. Basil, in painting and worshiping Dorian as the sensuous manifestation of his largely pure but tainted soul—the painting contains a tinge of evil—clearly suggests Rossetti, although he worships a beautiful boy instead of a beautiful lady.

In *The Renaissance*, however, Pater had presented the Victorian world with a new kind of artist, one who owed much to the Pre-Raphaelites but who could best be characterized as a decadent. Instead of painting and worshiping blessed, ethereal ladies, Pater's Leonardo—the type of the modern artist—had been fascinated, rather, by the head of the Medusa. Pater informs us of Leonardo's depiction of this terrible head: "The subject has been treated in various ways; Leonardo alone cuts to its centre; he alone realises it as the head of a corpse, exercising its powers through all the circumstances of death. What may be called the fascination of corruption penetrates in every touch its exquisitely finished beauty. About the dainty lines of the cheek the bat flits unheeded. The delicate snakes seem literally strangling each other in terrified struggle to escape from the Medusa brain." Leonardo plunged into the depths of "human personality and became above all a painter of portraits." In the bewitchingly evil, enigmatic, smiling face of the Mona Lisa, he found and captured on canvas the perfect expression of human personality as Pater felt the modern world has come to know it.

Insofar as one can generalize about the Pre-Raphaelite movement, it is possible to maintain that its fortunes after 1873 were on the decline. Rossetti, the chief Pre-Raphaelite, had two periods of intense creativity. The first occurred in the 1850s, the second around 1868. Most of the poems that comprise his masterpiece, *The House of Life*, were written between 1868 and 1870. However, Robert Buchanan's attack on him in "The Fleshly School of Poetry," which first appeared in the *Contemporary Review* in October, 1871, cut deep. Already "nervously debilitated, he now felt relentlessly persecuted by a whole Philistine world he had never cared to understand. Henceforth he was increasingly subject to delusive fears and more or less constant insomnia." He continued to write and paint until his death in 1882, and his reputation continued to spread as he attracted more and more disciples, but Rossetti himself was in a state of decline and no one of equal stature appeared to carry on the torch.

John Ruskin in another major figure one associates with the Pre-Raphaelites, though he was definitely separate from them. Ruskin was the chief promoter and defender of the early Pre-Raphaelites—Rossetti especially—and the author of the voluminous work, *Modern Painters* (1843–60), upon which the original Pre-Raphaelites looked with admiration. He fervently believed, moreover, that art and morality are inseparable. Richard Ellmann has observed of Basil: "The painter Hallward has little of Ruskin at the beginning [of *Dorian Gray*], but gradually he moves closer to that pillar of esthetic taste and moral judgment upon which Wilde leaned, and after Hallward is safely murdered, Dorian with sudden fondness recollects a trip they had made to Venice together, when his friend was captured by Tintoretto's art. Ruskin was of course the English discoverer and champion of Tintoretto, so that the allusion is specific."

In 1882, however, the youthful Oscar Wilde himself, speaking in the name of the new, amoral aesthetes of the 1880s, wrote that "we of the younger school have made a departure from the teachings of Mr. Ruskin,—a departure definite and different and decisive. . . . In his art criticism, his estimate of the joyous element of art, his whole method of approaching art, we are no longer with him; for the keystone to his aesthetic system is ethical always. He would judge of a picture by the amount of noble moral ideas it expresses." In the same essay—titled "L'Envoi"—Wilde declared that "the ultimate expression of our artistic movement in painting has been, not in the spiritual visions of the Pre-Raphaelites, for all their marvel of Greek legend and their mystery of Italian song, but in the work of such men as Whistler and Albert Moore, who have raised design and colour to the ideal level of poetry and music."

Wilde, in the essay, connects Ruskin with the Pre-Raphaelites and sees both as linking art with morality. Moreover, in 1878 Ruskin suffered the first of seven attacks of madness that culminated in 1889 with the most damaging one. Ruskin's recurring fits of insanity interfered seriously with his work, and after 1889 he wrote practically nothing and spent the rest of his life in mute retirement. As this was occurring, the decadent movement, sparked by *The Renaissance* and inspired from across the channel by writers such as Baudelaire, Verlaine, Mallarmé, and Huysmans, was gaining momentum. By 1890, it was clearly emerging as an important movement in literature, and the stage was set for the appearance of an Aubrey Beardsley in painting.

The steady deterioration of Basil Hallward as an artist between 1873 and the time of his death on a dark, foggy November night in 1889, is meant to symbolize the decline of Rosetti, Pre-Raphaelitism in general, and Ruskin's "Moral Aesthetic." At the beginning of *Dorian Gray*, Basil had made a request of Wotton: "Don't take away from me the one person who gives to my art whatever charm it possesses: my life as an artist depends on him." Wotton did not heed the request, and Basil's art consistently deteriorated as Dorian—symbol incarnate of the painter's soul—drifted away from him. It is not until Dorian reveals his true soul to Basil in the sinister thirteenth chapter of the novel, however, that the painter is completely destroyed as an artist:

> Hallward turned again to the portrait, and gazed at it. "My God, if it is true," he exclaimed, "and this is what you have done with your life, why, you must be worse even than those who talk against you fancy you to be!" He held the light up again to the canvas, and examined it. The surface seemed to be quite undisturbed, and as he had left it. It was from within, apparently, that the foulness and horror had come. Through some strange quickening of inner life the leprosies of sin were slowly eating the thing away. The rotting of a corpse in a watery grave was not so fearful.
>
> His hand shook, and the candle fell from its socket on the floor, and lay there sputtering. He placed his foot on it and put it out. Then he flung himself into the rickety chair that was standing by the table and buried his face in his hands.

Basil represents an art movement that recognizes the evil within the self and deals seriously with it, but can accept it only in small doses. When the soul reveals itself as overwhelmingly evil, Ruskin, or the Pre-Raphaelite artist, can only shrink away in horror and yield to the decadent, who can accept this vision and wring satisfaction from it. Basil's murder is not only the murder of one human being by another but also the murder of Pre-Raphaelite art and the Ruskinian "Moral Aesthetic" by decadent art. The horror on the canvas is specifically presented as an accomplice in the murder:

> Dorian Gray glanced at the picture, and suddenly an uncontrollable feeling of hatred for Basil Hallward came over him, as though it had been suggested to him by the image on the canvas, whispered into his ear by those grinning lips. The mad passions of a hunted animal stirred within him, and he loathed the man who was seated at the table, more than in his whole life he had ever loathed anything. . . . He rushed at him, and dug the knife into the great vein that is behind the ear, crushing the man's head down on the table, and stabbing again and again.

Dorian murders Basil because of an uncontrollable passion for sin, an insane desire to destroy the man who is praying and asking him to go down on his knees and pray too. The murder is an attempt on Dorian's part to stifle the voice of goodness forever. The picture's complicity in the murder, however, gives the act an added dimension: decadent art, having replaced Pre-Raphaelite art on the canvas and destroyed—even inverted—the Ruskinian link between art and morality, now completes the job by murdering the Pre-Raphaelite artist who, Ruskin-like, is praying to God. Quite probably, Wilde must have seen Ruskin's serious and very damaging attack of madness in the autumn of 1889 as effectively marking the end of an entire movement in art—certainly the end of the idea that art and morality are somehow wedded, an idea found not only in Ruskin but "in the spiritual visions of the Pre-Raphaelites" as well.

The murder of Basil is the turning point for Dorian. The portrait records this evil act, and Dorian begins to lose his nerve. The sight of so much evil becomes intolerable even to him, and he finds himself unable to derive pleasure from his new sin:

> He felt that if he brooded on what he had gone through he would sicken or grow mad. There were sins whose fascination was more in the memory than in the doing of them, strange triumphs that gratified the pride more than the passions, and gave to the intellect a quickened sense of joy, greater than any joy they brought, or could ever bring, to the senses. But this was not one of them. It was a thing to be driven out of the mind, to be drugged with poppies, to be strangled lest it might strangle one itself.

"Poppies" fail to strangle Dorian's sense of horror, though, and his encounter with Jim Vane shatters his nerves. The voice of goodness wells up from within him, poisoning his existence. He decides to escape by retracing his steps, by becoming once again a pure, innocent being, and his first good action is to spare a country girl. Wotton, however, suggests to him that the action was simply an attempt to experience a new sensation, and the portrait corroborates this by becoming more hideous. Dorian examines his motives closely and decides that this was indeed the case. Dorian, in this respect, is a typical decadent. Having yielded to the evil in himself, he ultimately discovers, to his horror, that he can no longer derive pleasure from it and that the plunge into the demon universe has become an irreversible process. Trapped in this demonic underworld, he has only one road of escape left, and that is death.

It is a road that Alan Campbell before him had taken. Alan had been corrupted by Dorian, but withdrew from a life of sin and decided to give expression to his corrupt impulses only within the framework of science, cutting up corpses and experimenting on rotting bodies. Dorian, however, brings him to a terrible and unbearable confrontation with evil—a confrontation Alan could not have possibly avoided—and the result is Alan's suicide. This is the inevitable end of the decadent, and Alan's suicide presages Dorian's death. Dorian, unable to bear the sight of his hideous portrait any longer, and identifying it with his conscience, decides to destroy it. For Dorian, this is the ultimate evil act, the desire to rid himself of all moral sense. The attempt to escape through good actions having failed, he decides to escape by committing the most terrible of crimes. When he plunges the blade into his "monstrous soul-life," however, he kills himself—this is really his only way out.

Wotton remains alive, but his fate, paradoxically, is the worst in the novel and is foreshadowed when his wife deserts him. Wotton's wife is not an individual but a type. Wilde says of her: "She was usually in love with somebody, and, as her passion was never returned, she had kept all her illusions. She tried to look picturesque, but only succeeded in being untidy. Her name was Victoria, and she had a perfect mania for going to church." She is the Victorian world personified, and Wotton's marriage to her is as necessary to his well-being as the dinner parties he attends. The paradoxist must have a fixed standard of values if he is to create paradoxes. Wotton as paradoxist continually stands Victorian values on their heads, but his marriage to Victoria is necessary if he is to continue to do this.

Unfortunately for Wotton, the continual process of inverting Victorian values ultimately destroys those values, and Victoria finally commits the very un-Victorian act of eloping. This, however, merely foreshadows Wotton's loss of his artistic masterpiece, Dorian, into whom he had poured all his soul. Wotton's paradoxes were only the means to an end—they were the evil brush he used to refashion Dorian in the light of his own soul. It should be stressed that Wotton has entirely renounced evil in his life, and has given full expression to the evil within himself only in his art. When Dorian dies, Wotton, the Satan-figure of *The Picture of Dorian Gray*, suffers the very terrible fate of losing his soul. In their last meeting before Dorian's suicide, Wotton speaks:

> "By the way, Dorian," he said, after a pause, " 'what does it profit a man if he gain the whole world and lose—how does the quotation run?—his own soul?' "
>
> The music jarred and Dorian Gray started, and stared at his friend. "Why do you ask me that, Harry?"
>
> "My dear fellow," said Lord Henry, elevating his eyebrows in surprise, "I asked you because I thought you might be able to give me an answer. That is all. I was going through the Park last Sunday, and close

by the Marble Arch there stood a little crowd of shabby-looking people listening to some vulgar street-preacher. As I passed by, I heard the man yelling out that question to his audience. It struck me as being rather dramatic. London is very rich in curious effects of that kind. A wet Sunday, an uncouth Christian in a mackintosh, a ring of sickly white faces under a broken roof of dripping umbrellas, and a wonderful phrase flung into the air by shrill, hysterical lips—it was really very good in its way, quite a suggestion. I thought of telling the prophet that Art had a soul, but that man had not. I am afraid, however, he would not have understood me."

What Wotton says is true primarily of himself. Lord Henry has placed his soul entirely in his art—in Dorian—and when Dorian dies he loses it. Wotton's terrible end is probably a jab at Pater, who was too timid to practice in any way what Wilde believed him to have preached.

The Picture of Dorian Gray is about the coming-of-age of Victorian art and attitudes. Wilde saw human nature in nineteenth-century England as rapidly plummeting from innocence into an awareness of the demon universe. Wotton is delighted by this. "The only people to whose opinions I listen with any respect," he says, "are people much younger than myself. They seem in front of me." Wilde's book mirrors this development, but it goes beyond that. The book contains a moral, as Wilde himself pointed out in a letter to the editor of the St. James's Gazette: "The moral is this: All excess, as well as all renunciation, brings its own punishment. The painter, Basil Hallward, worshipping physical beauty far too much, as most painters do, dies by the hand of one in whose soul he has created a monstrous and absurd vanity. Dorian Gray, having led a life of mere sensation and pleasure, tries to kill conscience, and at that moment kills himself. Lord Henry Wotton seeks to be merely the spectator of life. He finds that those who reject the battle are more deeply wounded than those who take part in it. Yes; there is a terrible moral in Dorian Gray."

Basil's attachment to the figure of Dorian—to his physical beauty and the purity it reflects—is extreme, and it destroys him, while Dorian's attempt to yield entirely to evil leads to his death. Wotton's rejection of evil in life is total, and he loses his soul but remains physically alive to endure the agonies of his spiritual damnation. What is needed, then, is a point of balance. One must neither completely renounce evil in life nor yield entirely to it. Wilde is counseling moderation in Dorian Gray: the Victorians are now deep in the demon universe, and unless they maintain a balance between good and evil, renunciation and excess, they will be destroyed.

This is true of life but not of art. In a second letter on Dorian Gray to the editor of the *St. James's Gazette,* Wilde wrote: "It is proper that limitations should be placed on action. It is not proper that limitations should be placed on art." In art, one can descend to the bottom of the demon universe and emerge unscathed. This is dramatized in the final pages of *The Picture of Dorian Gray.* Dorian's picture accompanies Dorian to the very depths of the demon universe, but it returns unharmed to its original state. Dorian, on the other hand, dies. The demonic, then, should be fully explored only in art, if the exploration is to remain a beautiful experience. *"The artist is the creator of beautiful things,"* Wilde wrote in the preface to *Dorian Gray,* and he also wrote that *"the artist can express everything."* An art that delves into the dark caverns of the soul and fully explores and celebrates the evil within can remain beautiful, but a way of life that seeks fully to translate inner evil into action will finally cease to be beautiful and become an inescapable nightmare. This is Wilde's position in *The Picture of Dorian Gray,* a position he never abandoned.

A biographical comment is inevitable at this point. Gone is the writer of fairy tales. Camelot is in ruins, and Wilde, now a habitual homosexual, is moving in the same direction as his protagonist, Dorian Gray. At the opening of the 1890s, Wilde was still convinced that he could escape disaster by maintaining a balance between renunciation and excess in his homosexual involvements. But in 1891 Lionel Johnson introduced him to Lord Alfred Douglas, soon to become the great passion of his life and for whose sake he was to abandon all restraint. It is fascinating that Dorian's fate prefigures Wilde's own: the novel suggests that Wilde probably had a presentiment of what the gods within had in store for him.

Chronology

1854	Born in Dublin on October 16.
1871–74	Student at Trinity College, Dublin.
1874–78	Student at Magdalen College, Oxford, where in 1878 he won the Newdigate Prize for poetry, and took a first-class degree in Classics and Humane Letters.
1884	Married to Constance Lloyd on May 29.
1887–89	Editorship of *The Woman's World*.
1891	Wilde's *annus mirabilis*. First meeting with his fatal love, Lord Alfred Douglas, a bad and rapacious poet. Publication of *The Picture of Dorian Gray*, *Intentions*, *Lord Arthur Savile's Crime* and *A House of Pomegranates*.
1892	*Lady Windermere's Fan*: first performance on February 20.
1893	*Salome* published. *A Woman of No Importance* performed.
1895	*An Ideal Husband* first performed on January 3, and Wilde's masterpiece, *The Importance of Being Earnest* first performed on February 14. Wilde sued the Marquis of Queensberry, Lord Alfred Douglas' father, for libel. The trial, April 3–5, resulted in the Marquis' acquital. This was followed by two trials of Wilde himself on criminal charges of homosexuality. The first, April 26 to May 1, ended in a hung jury, but the second, May 20–25, resulted in Wilde's conviction and subsequent imprisonment for two years of hard labor.
1897	Writes *De Profundis* in Reading Gaol as a letter to Lord Alfred Douglas. Departs for France on May 19, upon release from prison.
1898	*The Ballad of Reading Gaol* published.
1900	Death in Paris on November 30, at the age of just forty-six.

Contributors

HAROLD BLOOM, Sterling Professor of the Humanities at Yale University, is the author of *The Anxiety of Influence, Poetry and Repression* and many other volumes of literary criticism. His forthcoming study, *Freud: Transference and Authority*, attempts a full-scale reading of all of Freud's major writings. He is the general editor of *The Chelsea House Library of Literary Criticism*.

WILLIAM BUTLER YEATS, the Irish poet and playwright, is universally acknowledged as the greatest poet of our language in this century. His strongest achievements were in the volumes, *The Tower, The Winding Stair* and perhaps also in his *Last Poems and Plays*.

ERIC BENTLEY is widely regarded as one of the foremost literary critics of modern drama. His books include *The Playwright as Thinker*. He is currently Professor of Comparative Literature at the University of Maryland.

EDOUARD RODITI is an internationally known man-of-letters, who has achieved recognition as a poet, essayist and writer of fiction.

G. WILSON KNIGHT is one of the foremost literary critics of this century. Now retired from his professorship at the University of Leeds, he continues to be active as a lecturer, and as a dramatic director and performer. Best known for his critical books on Shakespeare, including *The Wheel of Fire* and *The Imperial Theme*, he is equally eminent in his studies of romanticism and poetic tradition, including *The Starlit Dome, The Burning Oracle* and *The Christian Renaissance*.

EPIFANIO SAN JUAN, JR. is Professor of English at the University of Connecticut, Storrs.

RICHARD ELLMANN, formerly Goldsmiths Professor of English at New College, Oxford, is now Research Professor at Emory University. Perhaps the leading modern literary biographer, he is best known for his books on Joyce and Yeats. His long-awaited biography of Oscar Wilde promises to be the definitive study.

CHRISTOPHER S. NASSAAR is Professor of English at the American University in Beirut.

Bibliography

Beckson, Karl, ed. *Oscar Wilde: The Critical Heritage*. London: Routledge and Kegan Paul, 1970.

Bird Alan. *The Plays of Oscar Wilde*. London: Vision, 1977.

Cohen, Philip K. *The Moral Vision of Oscar Wilde*. London: Associated University Press, 1978.

Douglas, Alfred Lord. *Oscar Wilde: A Summing Up*. London: Gerald Duckworth, 1940.

Ellmann, Richard. "Romantic Pantomime in Oscar Wilde." *Partisan Review* 30 (Fall 1963): 342–55.

———, ed. *Oscar Wilde: A Collection of Critical Essays*. Englewood Cliffs, N.J.: Prentice-Hall, 1969.

———, ed. *The Artist as Critic: Critical Writings of Oscar Wilde*. New York: Random House, 1968.

Ericksen, Donald H. *Oscar Wilde*. Boston: Twayne Publishers, 1977.

Ervine, John. *Oscar Wilde*. New York: William Morrow and Co., 1952.

Gide, André. *Oscar Wilde: In Memoriam*. New York: Philosophical Library, 1949.

Harris, Frank. *Oscar Wilde: His Life and Confessions*. New York: Harrison Press, 1974.

Hart-Davis, Rupert, ed. *The Letters of Oscar Wilde*. New York: Harcourt, Brace and World, Inc., 1962.

Hough, Graham. *The Last Romantics*. London: Gerald Duckworth, 1949.

Hyde, H. Montgomery. *Oscar Wilde: A Biography*. New York: Da Capo Press, 1975.

Jullian, Philippe. *Oscar Wilde*. Translated by Violet Wyndham. New York: Viking, 1969.

Morely, Sheriden. *Oscar Wilde*. New York: Holt, Rinehart and Winston, 1976.

Murray, Isobel, ed. *The Complete Shorter Fiction of Oscar Wilde*. Oxford: Oxford University Press, 1968.

Nassaar, Christopher S. *Into the Demon Universe: A Literary Exploration of Oscar Wilde*. New Haven: Yale University Press, 1974.

Pearson, Hesketh. *Oscar Wilde: His Life and Wit*. New York: Harper and Brothers, 1946.

Roditi, Edouard. *Oscar Wilde*. Norfolk, Conn.: New Directions Books, 1947.

San Juan, Epifanio, Jr. *The Art of Oscar Wilde*. Princeton: Princeton University Press, 1967.

Sherman, Rodney. *Oscar Wilde: Art and Egotism*. London: Macmillan, 1977.

Sullivan, Kevin. *Oscar Wilde*. New York: Columbia University Press, 1972.

Symons, Arthur. *A Study of Oscar Wilde.* London: Charles J. Sawyer, 1930.

Weintraub, Stanley, ed. *The Literary Criticism of Oscar Wilde.* Lincoln: University of Nebraska Press, 1968.

Winwar, Frances. *Oscar Wilde and the Yellow 'Nineties.* New York: Harper and Brothers, 1940.

Acknowledgments

"The Tragic Generation: Wilde" by William Butler Yeats from *Autobiography* by William Butler Yeats, copyright © 1916, 1936 by The Macmillan Company, renewed 1944 by Bertha Georgie Yeats. Reprinted by permission.

"The Importance of Being Earnest" by Eric Bentley from *The Playwright as Thinker* by Eric Bentley, copyright © 1946 by Eric Bentley. Reprinted by permission of Harcourt, Brace, Jovanovich, Inc.

"The Poems in Prose" by Edouard Roditi from *Oscar Wilde* by Edouard Roditi, copyright © 1947 by New Directions Publishing Corporation. Reprinted by permission of New Directions.

"Christ and Wilde" by G. Wilson Knight from *The Christian Renaissance* by G. Wilson Knight, copyright © 1962 by G. Wilson Knight. Reprinted by permission of W. W. Norton and Co., Inc.

"The Action of the Comedies" by Epifanio San Juan, Jr., from *The Art of Oscar Wilde* by Epifanio San Juan, Jr., copyright © 1967 by Princeton University Press. Reprinted by permission of Princeton University Press.

"Overtures to *Salome*" by Richard Ellmann from *Yearbook of Comparative and General Literature* 17 (1968), and *Tri-Quarterly*, copyright © 1968 by *Yearbook of Comparative and General Literature* and by *Tri-Quarterly* for the revisions made in the original article. Reprinted by permission.

"The Critic as Artist as Wilde" by Richard Ellmann from *The Artist as Critic: Critical Writings of Oscar Wilde*, edited by Richard Ellmann, copyright © 1968, 1969 by Richard Ellmann. Reprinted by permission of Random House, Inc.

"The Darkening Lens" by Christopher S. Nassaar from *Into the Demon Universe: A Literary Exploration of Oscar Wilde*, copyright © 1974 by Yale University Press. Reprinted by permission of Yale University Press.

Index